FOREWORD

This publication has been prepared under our direction for use by our respective commands and other commands as appropriate.

DAVID A. FASTABEND
Brigadier General, US Army
Deputy Director/Chief of Staff
  Futures Center
US Army Training and doctrine
  Command

THOMAS L. CONANT
Brigadier General, USMC
Director
Capabilities Development Directorate
Marine Corps Combat Development
  Command

JOHN M. KELLY
Rear Admiral, USN
Commander
Navy Warfare Development
  Command

BENTLEY B. RAYBURN
Major General, USAF
Commander
Headquarters Air Force
    Doctrine Center

This publication is available through the ALSA Web site (www.alsa.mil); through the Army at Army Knowledge Online (AKO) (www.us.army.mil) and at the General Dennis J. Reimer Training and Doctrine Digital Library (www.train.army.mil) Web sites; and through the Air Force at the Air Force Publishing Web site (www.e-publishing.af.mil).

PREFACE

1. Purpose

This publication identifies standard tactics, techniques, and procedures (TTP) among the Services for planning, integrating, and executing explosive ordnance disposal (EOD) operations in a joint environment. It sets forth TTP to assist joint activities and performance of the entire EOD force and establishes the procedures necessary to protect all United States (US) military and multinational personnel and operations.

2. Scope

This multi-Service tactics, techniques, and procedures (MTTP) manual provides guidance and procedures for the employment of an EOD force when operating in a joint capacity throughout the range of military operations.

3. Applicability

This publication applies to all leaders, planners, and the EOD warfighter when deploying forces into any theater. The TTP established in this manual apply to the commanders of combatant commands, subunified commands, joint task forces (JTFs), and subordinate components of these commands.

4. Implementation Plan

Participating Service command offices of primary responsibility (OPRs) will review this publication, validate the information, and reference and incorporate it in Service and command manuals, regulations, and curricula as follows:

Army. Upon approval and authentication, this publication incorporates the procedures contained herein into the US Army Doctrine and Training Literature Program as directed by the Commander, US Army Training and Doctrine Command (TRADOC). Distribution is in accordance with applicable directives and the Initial Distribution Number (IDN) listed on the authentication page.

Marine Corps. The Marine Corps will incorporate the procedures in this publication in US Marine Corps training and doctrine publications as directed by the Commanding General, US Marine Corps Combat Development Command (MCCDC). Distribution is in accordance with the Marine Corps Publication Distribution System (MCPDS).

Navy. The Navy will incorporate these procedures in US Navy training and doctrine publications as directed by the Commander, Navy Warfare Development Command (NWDC)[N5]. Distribution is in accordance with Military Standard Requisition and Issue Procedure Desk Guide (MILSTRIP Desk Guide) Navy Supplement Publication-409 (NAVSUP P-409).

Air Force. The Air Force will incorporate the procedures in this publication in accordance with applicable governing directives. Distribution is in accordance with Air Force Instruction (AFI) 33-360.

Marine Corps PCN: 144 000096 00

5. User Information

a. TRADOC, MCCDC, NWDC, Headquarters Air Force Doctrine Center (AFDC), and the Air Land Sea Application (ALSA) Center developed this publication with the joint participation of the approving Service commands. ALSA will review and update this publication as necessary.

b. This publication reflects current joint and Service doctrine, command and control organizations, facilities, personnel, responsibilities, and procedures. Changes in Service protocol, appropriately reflected in joint and Service publications, will likewise be incorporated in revisions to this document.

c. We encourage recommended changes for improving this publication. Key your comments to the specific page and paragraph and provide a rationale for each recommendation. Send comments and recommendations directly to—

Army

Commander
US Army Training and Doctrine Command
ATTN: ATFC-RD
Fort Monroe VA 23651-5000
DSN 680-3951 COMM (757) 788-3951
E-mail: doctrine@monroe.army.mil

Marine Corps

Commanding General
US Marine Corps Combat Development Command
ATTN: C427
3300 Russell Road, Suite 318A
Quantico VA 22134-5021
DSN 278-2871/6227 COMM (703) 784-2871/6227
E-mail: deputydirectordoctrine@usmc.mil

Navy

Commander
Navy Warfare Development Command
ATTN: N5
686 Cushing Road
Newport RI 02841-1207
DSN 948-1164/4189 COMM (401) 841-1164/4189
E-mail: alsapubs@nwdc.navy.mil

Air Force

HQ AFDC/DJ
155 North Twining Street
Maxwell AFB AL 36112-6112
DSN 493-2640/2256 COMM: (334) 953-2640/2256
E-mail: afdc.dj@maxwell.af.mil

ALSA

ALSA Center
ATTN: Director
114 Andrews Street
Langley AFB VA 23665-2785
DSN 575-0902 COMM (757) 225-0902
E-mail: alsa.director@langley.af.mil

*FM 4-30.16
MCRP 3-17.2C
NTTP 3-02.5
AFTTP(I) 3-2.32

FM 4-30.16   US Army Training and Doctrine Command
                                                                Fort Monroe, Virginia

MCRP 3-17.2C   Marine Corps Combat Development Command
                                                                  Quantico, Virginia

NTTP 3-02.5   Navy Warfare Development Command
                                                                Newport, Rhode Island

AFTTP(I) 3-2.32   Headquarters, Air Force Doctrine Center
                                                          Maxwell Air Force Base, Alabama

27 October 2005

EOD

MULTI-SERVICE TACTICS, TECHNIQUES, AND PROCEDURES FOR EXPLOSIVE ORDNANCE DISPOSAL IN A JOINT ENVIRONMENT

TABLE OF CONTENTS

TABLES

EXECUTIVE SUMMARY

EOD

Multi-Service Tactics, Techniques, and Procedures for Explosive Ordnance Disposal in a Joint Environment

This manual –

- Describes Service-specific EOD organizations, capabilities, equipment, doctrine, and training.
- Provides joint EOD command and control (C2) considerations.
- Provides guidance for planning and conducting EOD operations in a joint environment.
- Establishes procedures for information management (IM) and operational and intelligence reporting.

Introduction

This publication documents the C2 considerations and procedures for conducting EOD operations in a joint environment. These TTP are necessary to coordinate and integrate multi-Service EOD operations to facilitate efficient and safe joint EOD operations. The EOD force performed in a joint capacity during many recent operations; however, most of the command relationships and coordination requirements were ad hoc. Each Service routinely deploys EOD forces into a theater and assigns the force based on Service needs rather than the theater needs as a whole. This MTTP provides many considerations for employing EOD forces in a joint capacity and provides C2 options for the geographic combatant commander and commander, joint task force (CJTF) to consider. This MTTP also highlights the EOD capabilities and force structures for each Service.

Concept and Organization

Chapters I and II highlight the significant joint C2 issues when preparing to employ EOD forces. The focus of the Service chapters (chapters III-VI) is for the benefit of non-EOD commanders and staff and EOD commanders and staff from other Services to gain an understanding of the personnel/equipment and doctrine utilized within the other Services. Finally, in an effort to expedite C2 requirements for the senior theater EOD commander, the MTTP offers standardized EOD reporting formats which each Service has agreed to use when operating in a joint environment. Countering unexploded explosive ordnance (UXO) and the threat it creates during all operations is challenging. This MTTP provides the necessary command structure to assist (rather than impair) efficient EOD operations. This challenge becomes easier as the level of knowledge regarding other Services' EOD forces and their contributions to the mission increase.

Command and Control

By capturing methods used to coordinate joint EOD operations, this publication offers three command relationship options in how to best employ the entire EOD force:

- Service-component responsibility (with direct liaison authorized [DIRLAUTH]).

- Lead-Service component (with or without tactical control [TACON] or operational control [OPCON] of other Service EOD forces).

- Subordinate EOD Joint Task Force (EOD JTF).

Other C2 considerations when utilizing these task organization options include:

a. The geographic combatant commander or CJTF can modify or mix these options to the theater mission, threat, and situation.

b. This MTTP publication establishes methods for creating a joint EOD operations center (JEODOC) to assist and streamline the management of EOD operations at a single command, normally under the direction of the J-3.

c. The JEODOC is useful whenever joint EOD management requirements are beyond the capability of the J-4 and/or the subordinate EOD force headquarters. Both the Army and Navy have existing C2 EOD units around which a JEODOC or EOD JTF headquarters can be built. Specifically, the Army's battalion (O-5 command) and group (O-6 command) headquarters, or the Navy's Mobile Unit (O-5 command) and group (O-6 command), provide a ready EOD headquarters unit to quickly manage or command joint EOD operations.

Chapters

Chapter I – Introduces the Department of Defense (DOD) EOD mission, capabilities, and common characteristics of the EOD force. This chapter also provides a historical perspective of EOD operations and the impact the threat has had on US operations.

Chapter II – Describes the purpose for conducting EOD operations as a joint force, provides historical examples, and employment options for the joint force commander (JFC) to consider when employing EOD forces. This chapter also provides guidance for standing up a JEODOC.

Chapter III – Discusses Army EOD operations to include the Army EOD mission, Service doctrine, Army organizations and capabilities, and specific Army EOD training.

Chapter IV – Discusses Marine Corps EOD operations to include the Marine Corps EOD mission, Service doctrine, Marine Corps organizations and capabilities, and specific Marine Corps EOD training.

Chapter V – Discusses Navy EOD operations to include the Navy EOD mission, Service doctrine, Navy EOD organizations and capabilities, and specific Navy EOD training.

Chapter VI – Discusses Air Force EOD operations to include Air Force EOD mission, Service doctrine, Air Force organizations and capabilities, and specific Air Force EOD training.

Appendices

Appendix A – Offers a multi-Service EOD capabilities matrix for commanders and planners to understand what capabilities each Service can and cannot provide.

Appendix B – Provides a CJTF staff or EOD staff officer with a logical checklist of necessary EOD planning requirements during each stage of an operation.

Appendix C – Describes the procedures for standing up an EOD JTF and the responsibilities of each Service's EOD force. Also identifies EOD-specific EOD JTF staff requirements and provides an example of a notional EOD JTF staff.

Appendix D – Formulates and describes the required EOD reports and standardizes reporting requirements when operating in a joint environment.

Appendix E – Captures the recurring EOD operations each Service routinely conducts.

PROGRAM PARTICIPANTS

The following commands and agencies participated in the development of this publication:

Joint

DOD EOD Technology and Training Secretariat, Indian Head, MD
Joint Warfighting Center, Fort Monroe, VA
Joint Staff, J-34, Combating Terrorism, Washington, DC
Commandant, Naval School EOD, Eglin AFB, FL

Army

HQ, DA, ATTN: DALO-AMA-EOD, Washington, DC
HQ, TRADOC, Futures Center, Requirements Directorate, Joint and Allied Doctrine
    Division (ATFC-RD), Fort Monroe, VA
US Army Pacific, ATTN: EODCT, Fort Shafter, HI
TRADOC Munitions System Manager, Redstone Arsenal, AL
HQ, 52d Ordnance Group (EOD), Fort Gillem, GA
HQ, 79th Ordnance Battalion (EOD), Fort Sam Houston, TX
HQ, 184th Ordnance Battalion (EOD), Fort Gillem, GA
US Army Technical Detachment, NAVEODTECHDIV, Indian Head, MD
Army EOD Training Representative, Fort Lee, VA
Army Engineer School, Fort Leonard Wood, MO

Marine Corps

Marine Corps Combat Development Command, Joint Doctrine Branch (C427) and
    Ground Branch (C422), Quantico, VA
Marine Corps Detachment, Naval School EOD (NAVSCOLEOD), Eglin AFB, FL
Marine Corps Detachment, Naval EOD Technology Division (NAVEODTECHDIV),
    Indian Head, MD
HQ, USMC LPE, (EOD Advocacy), Washington, DC
2d Marine Air Wing, Cherry Point, NC
I Marine Expeditionary Force, Camp Pendleton, CA
II Marine Expeditionary Force, Camp Lejeune, NC
MCAS Miramar, COMCAB West, CA
MCAS Cherry Point COMCAB EAST, NC

Navy

NWDC, ALSA Liaison Officer (LNO), Norfolk Naval Base, Norfolk, VA
Commander, Maritime Force Protection Command, Norfolk, VA

Commander, EOD Group ONE, San Diego, CA
Commander, EOD Group TWO, Norfolk, VA

Air Force

HQ USAF/CE, Washington, DC
HQ Air Force Doctrine Center, Maxwell AFB, AL
HQ Air Combat Command, CE/EOD Division, Langley AFB, VA
Air Force CE Support Agency, Tyndall AFB, FL
HQ Air Force Special Operations Command, CE/EOD Division, Hurlburt Field, FL
HQ Air Force Materiel Command, CE/EOD Division, Wright-Patterson AFB, OH
HQ Air Force Space Command, CE/EOD Division, Peterson AFB, CO

HQ Air Mobility Command, CE/EOD Division, Scott AFB, MO
HQ Air Education Training Command, CE/EOD Division, Randolph AFB, TX
HQ United States Air Forces in Europe, CE/EOD Division, Ramstein AFB, GE
HQ Pacific Air Forces, CE/EOD Division, Hickam AFB, HI
56th CE Squadron, Luke AFB, AZ
75th CE Group, Hill AFB, UT
HQ United States Central Command Air Forces, USAF EOD Liaison Officer, Tampa, FL
Detachment 63, Aircraft and Armament Center, Indian Head, MD
HQ Air Force Reserve Command, CE/EOD Division, Robins AFB, GA

Chapter I

EOD WITHIN THE DEPARTMENT OF DEFENSE

1. Mission

The mission of DOD EOD is to support the JFC to neutralize hazards from foreign and domestic, conventional, chemical, biological, radiological, nuclear, high-yield explosives (CBRNE) UXO and improvised explosive devices (IEDs) that present a threat to operations, installations, personnel, or materiel.

2. Threat

The increasing potential of UXO resulting from the proliferation of arms, ammunition, and explosives throughout the world, coupled with the increasing asymmetric nature of the threat, provide a significant challenge to the JFC to ensure the mobility and survivability of the joint force. Area denial-type munitions containing anti-disturbance, influence, self-destruct, remote control, booby-trap, or contact fuzing also directly threaten US forces. The increasing availability of CBRNE material, components, and weapons raises the possibility of terrorists using these weapons, or conventional IEDs, in an attack against civilian populations or military facilities and units. Wherever US forces operate, these threats exist.

3. Capabilities

Military EOD personnel and equipment provide a variety of capabilities to commanders. Joint regulations and DOD directives prescribe specific responsibilities for each Service. Common EOD training, equipment, and technical manuals provide each Service with the capability to detect, identify, field evaluate, render safe, recover, and make final disposition of conventional or CBRNE UXO and IEDs, both foreign and domestic. Due to specific training and safety measures, equipment capabilities, and technical issues, only EOD-qualified personnel can provide safe and effective EOD support to US military operations. See Appendix A, "Multi-Service EOD Capabilities Matrix," and the individual Service chapters (chapters III-VI) for a detailed listing of specific Service EOD capabilities.

4. Common Characteristics

a. History. The development of the US military EOD force was an outgrowth of the bitter experience of the British at the beginning of World War II, when the Germans dropped thousands of bombs and mines containing large explosive charges on land and in the waters around Great Britain. The US started an EOD Service shortly before entering World War II by sending representatives from each of the military branches to England for bomb disposal training. Those representatives returned to the US and established separate Army and Navy bomb disposal schools. By 1960, DOD combined the Army and Navy schools under Navy cognizance to become the Naval School EOD. In 1971, DOD designated the Secretary of the Navy as the single manager for EOD technology and training.

b. Multi-Service EOD School. The Naval School EOD (NAVSCOLEOD) located at Eglin AFB, FL, is a Navy command, staffed by Army, Navy, Air Force, and Marine Corps instructors. The EOD course of instruction is approximately 6 months in length for Army, Air Force, and Marine Corps personnel and 12 months long for Navy personnel. Navy personnel receive additional instruction in diving procedures and underwater ordnance operations. NAVSCOLEOD trains officer and enlisted personnel from all Services in munitions identification, render-safe procedures, explosives safety, and EOD-unique equipment. The school's mission is to provide EOD-trained individuals to the operating forces of all US Services and to provide training to various federal agencies and international students.

c. EOD Research and Development. The Navy is assigned as the single manager for all DOD EOD research and development, training and evaluation, and common-type training. The Naval EOD Technology Division (NAVEODTECHDIV), Indian Head, MD, is a Navy command with collocated detachments of all Services, which is responsible for research and development of specialized EOD tools, equipment, techniques, and procedures common to two or more Services. This research and development assists EOD units in maintaining a modern capability to detect/locate, render safe, or dispose of UXO and associated hazards. All Services can submit requirements to the NAVEODTECHDIV for equipment development and can provide input to the prioritization and selection of projects for development. The Services also provide final approval and acceptance of developed items.

d. EOD Technical Manuals. All Services use the same EOD technical manuals as the basis for EOD training and technical procedures. The NAVEODTECHDIV develops and publishes these technical manuals and receives joint Service input and approval prior to publication. The NAVEODTECHDIV limits access to EOD publications to EOD-qualified personnel who are performing EOD duties. The NAVEODTECHDIV regularly exchanges information with both US national agencies and allied ordnance experts to stay abreast of the latest UXO trends and threats.

e. Common Equipment. All military EOD teams possess the same basic EOD tools to detect, identify, evaluate, render safe, and perform final disposition of explosive devices and associated hazards. These tools include portable x-ray equipment, robots, specialized demolition charges, and specialized tools for removing fuzes. Each Service has specialized EOD equipment to perform Service-unique EOD missions.

5. Interoperability

The existing multi-Service training and technical manuals, common equipment, and jointly supported research and development program make EOD one of the most interoperable specialties in the US military. Multi-Service EOD forces have worked side by side in numerous operations during recent contingencies and conflicts. These joint EOD operations demonstrate the potential for greater planning and operational efficiency in the future.

Chapter II

EOD IN A JOINT ENVIRONMENT

1. Operations

a.   Background. UXO and other hazardous devices (e.g., IED) in a theater of operations will likely threaten military forces and operations. US personnel have been killed or injured by UXO/IED in virtually every conflict or contingency in which the US has participated. The UXO/IED threat is even more serious to non-military members of the force (e.g., DOD civilians and contractor personnel) and other civilians located in the operational area since these individuals are unfamiliar with military ordnance. While Service components usually deploy with, and are supported by, their own EOD assets, the number of these assets is very limited and in high demand. In many situations, the geographic combatant commanders, through their directive authority for logistics, can achieve economy of effort by organizing their EOD forces using common servicing. Common servicing may allow the JFC to provide more efficient and effective EOD support to the joint force depending on the operational scenario. The JFC should also include integration of coalition/alliance, host nation and/or contracted EOD forces in a joint/multinational EOD task force.

Note: Other sources of EOD forces are not always trained to the same high standards as US EOD forces. When contracting out EOD support, the JFC contracting officer must take special care to ensure that commercial EOD firms meet an acceptable level standard of training and equipment as determined by US military EOD experts.

---

b.   Historical Examples. During previous US contingencies/operations, EOD assets from different Services combined their efforts to maximize the efficiency of EOD operations. While effective, most were accomplished in an ad hoc manner, often improvised on site between the local EOD commanders.

(1) Operation DESERT STORM. During the major UXO cleanup effort in Kuwait immediately after Desert Storm, EOD forces from each of the Services were organized into a de facto subordinate EOD JTF under Task Force Freedom. The JTF dealt with the large numbers of UXO remaining in Kuwait City. This organizational technique allowed the task force and subordinate EOD commanders to focus all available EOD assets on the major UXO clean-up effort in an organized and efficient manner, thus reducing the need for individual Services to bring more EOD assets into the country.

(2) Somalia. In Somalia, EOD forces from the Army, Air Force, and Marines operated together to remove UXO by sharing response sectors in Mogadishu. Navy EOD personnel supplemented Army EOD soldiers in destroying captured enemy ammunition (CEA) at an improvised demolition range.

(3) Bosnia. In support of continued peacekeeping efforts in Bosnia, US EOD forces were integrated to provide EOD services for the elimination of UXO and to support conventional/special operations and coalition forces.

(4) Operations ENDURING FREEDOM/IRAQI FREEDOM. During major UXO/IED/CEA efforts in these areas, EOD assets from all the Services combined their efforts to maximize the effectiveness of EOD operations.

c. Planning. A common servicing approach for EOD support is often the most efficient means to address the UXO/IED threat, especially when a limited number of EOD forces are available. Factors affecting the structure of a joint EOD force include intelligence and terrorist threats, parent unit mission (e.g., flight operations, demining, or support to special operations forces [SOF]). Appendix B, "EOD Planning Checklist for Joint Operations," provides general EOD planning guidance to support contingency operations. The JFC at all levels should have an EOD staff cell in their Plans/Operations Center.

2. Employment Options

a. Background. The magnitude of the UXO/IED threat in the joint operations area (JOA), coupled with the overall operational situation, normally determines the value added and degree of common servicing desired for EOD support.

b. JFC Options. This chapter provides three options for structuring a joint EOD force to accomplish the theater mission. Each option and organizational example depict the use of Service forces to accomplish the EOD mission. If the geographic combatant commander uses a functional command structure for the theater, the JFC operations directorate of a joint staff (J-3) would still have overall responsibility, with Service forces performing the EOD mission. In each organizational option, there should be a 24/7 joint EOD operations center (JEODOC) established. Based on the situation, the CJTF can modify or mix any of the following options:

(1) Service-component responsibility (with DIRLAUTH).

(2) Lead-Service component (with or without TACON or OPCON) of other Service EOD forces.

(3) Subordinate EOD JTF.

c. Forming a JEODOC. All JTFs, possibly even up to the sub-unified command-level, should have a JEODOC to track and coordinate JOA-wide EOD support. The JEODOC would be formed from existing major EOD commands such as an Army's battalion (O-5 command) and group (O-6 command) headquarters or the Navy's mobile unit (O-5 command) and group (O-6 command). In every case, other Service EOD staff officers and noncommissioned officers would augment the primary Service EOD staff.

d. JEODOC Functions. The JEODOC operating under the JTF J-3, or lead Service operations staff, or as part of the EOD JTF J-3 staff, provides oversight over all EOD operations in theater, tracks critical EOD assets, monitors and recommends changes in priorities, and resolves issues between Service components. Its primary purpose is to manage theater-level UXO/IED hazard-reduction operations and EOD planning, integrating, coordinating, and tasking functions (through the direction and authority of the commander). When not part of an EOD JTF, the JEODOC tasking authority enables the JTF to change Service-component EOD force responsibilities as the operation transitions through different phases. This allows Service EOD support to increase or decrease based upon operational tempo or the theater EOD mission. The major functions resident in the JEODOC are:

(1) Operations Section. This section monitors, synchronizes, and reports EOD operations to ensure maximum efficiency throughout the JOA. It ensures current theater-EOD operations are synchronized with CJTF intent. It develops and maintains the operational needs statement and manages the Army Corps of Engineers EOD cell that controls all contracted EOD support.

(2) Intelligence Section. This section also monitors and interprets the enemy and friendly situation for the commander and informs forces of significant changes in operations, objectives, and priorities.

(3) Administrative/Logistics (Admin/Log) Section. The admin/log section identifies immediate or potential problems in the support or materiel system. This section determines logistics support resource requirements, coordinates airlift requests, and special transportation requirements, and provides feedback (on request) for mission-essential repair and support items.

(4) Communications-Electronics Section. This section provides information systems planning, coordination, and support to the JEODOC and all joint, multinational, and external organizations, as required.

3. Service Component Responsibility with DIRLAUTH Option

a. Utilization. The Service-component responsibility employment option is used when each Service component provides for and controls its own EOD forces and requirements. In this option, DIRLAUTH would be authorized between the senior EOD command of each Service component which allows the local EOD commander to support other Service requirements on a case-by-case basis (figure II-1). Historically, this has been the most common method of employing EOD forces, although this organizational option often does not provide the most effective or balanced use of EOD assets across the entire JOA.

b. Benefits and Drawbacks.

(1) Benefits.

(a) The Service component's EOD responsibilities are relatively clear and easy to control within their area of operations (AO) and/or bases.

(b) Allows Service components direct control of their own Service EOD forces.

(c) Allows the local EOD commander to provide EOD support to other Service component forces (per the owning Service component commander's priorities/requirements).

(2) Drawbacks.

(a) May cause severe inequities in EOD support for different forces or areas within a JOA.

(b) Lack of JFC control and reduced flexibility in meeting critical/unexpected EOD requirements that cross Service component lines.

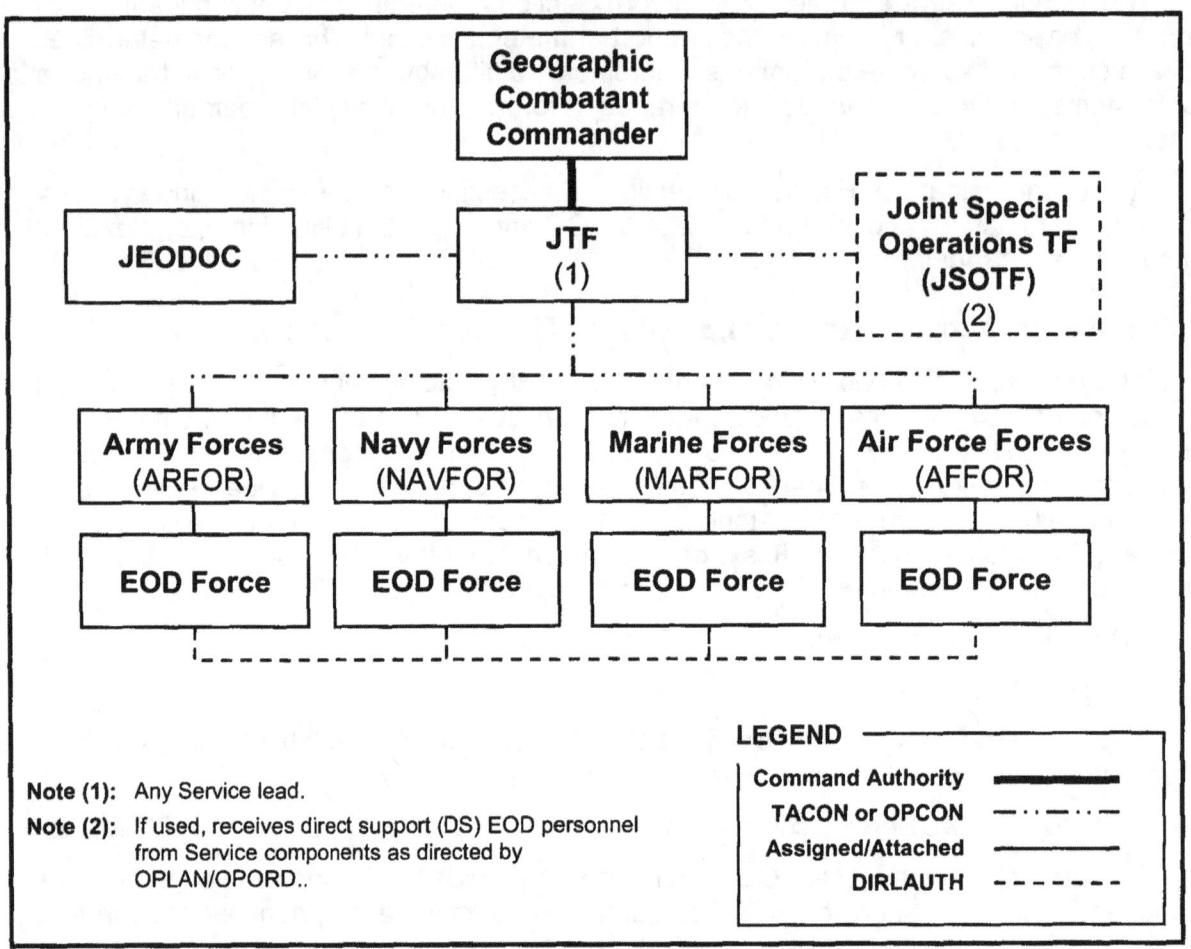

Figure II-1. Service Component Responsibility (with DIRLAUTH) Organization

4. Lead-Service Component (with or without TACON or OPCON) Option

a. Utilization. The combatant commander may use the lead-Service component option to support a limited duration mission or to provide more efficient EOD support, especially in a short notice, austere environment mission. In this option, the combatant commander, through his Title 10 authority, attaches specific EOD personnel to a specific Service-component with or without TACON/OPCON of other Services' EOD forces (figure II-2).

b. Formation. To establish a lead-Service component, the combatant commander, in consultation with his/her subordinate JFC and Service-component commanders, assigns specific common EOD tasks to a lead-Service component. Normally, the lead-Service component for EOD functions is the Service component with the majority of EOD requirements and capabilities in theater. The combatant commander may temporarily place selected EOD assets from one or more of the other Service components TACON or OPCON to the lead-Service component EOD commander to assist in accomplishing the assigned tasks. In this organizational option, the JEODOC may be formed and operated under the control of the lead Service. In any case, other Services providing forces to the lead Service should provide, or be directed to provide, staff augmentation (e.g., liaison officers [LNOs]) to the lead-Service EOD commander's staff. Having the JEODOC under the lead Service expedites planning, coordination, and mission execution. This option must include a support relationship for administrative/logistics support.

c. Employment Considerations. The lead-Service component option:

(1) Allows more efficient use of limited EOD assets for JTF-specific missions of limited duration or high priority. This option is not used to provide EOD support for specific Service-related missions (to include aircraft support, harbor clearances, and carrier battle-group support). Each Service retains select EOD forces to accomplish Service-specific missions.

(2) Centralizes JEODOC functions to include EOD operation taskings and data tracking with a single point of contact (POC), normally the lead-Service component EOD unit operations officer.

(3) Improves technical intelligence acquisition and dissemination to all EOD forces.

(4) May benefit the JFC and staff by placing the JEODOC function under the lead Service to assist in managing the EOD mission.

(5) Provides a mechanism that plans for fluctuations of Service EOD force responsibilities as the operation transitions through different phases. Allows Service EOD support to increase or decrease based on operational tempo or the theater EOD mission.

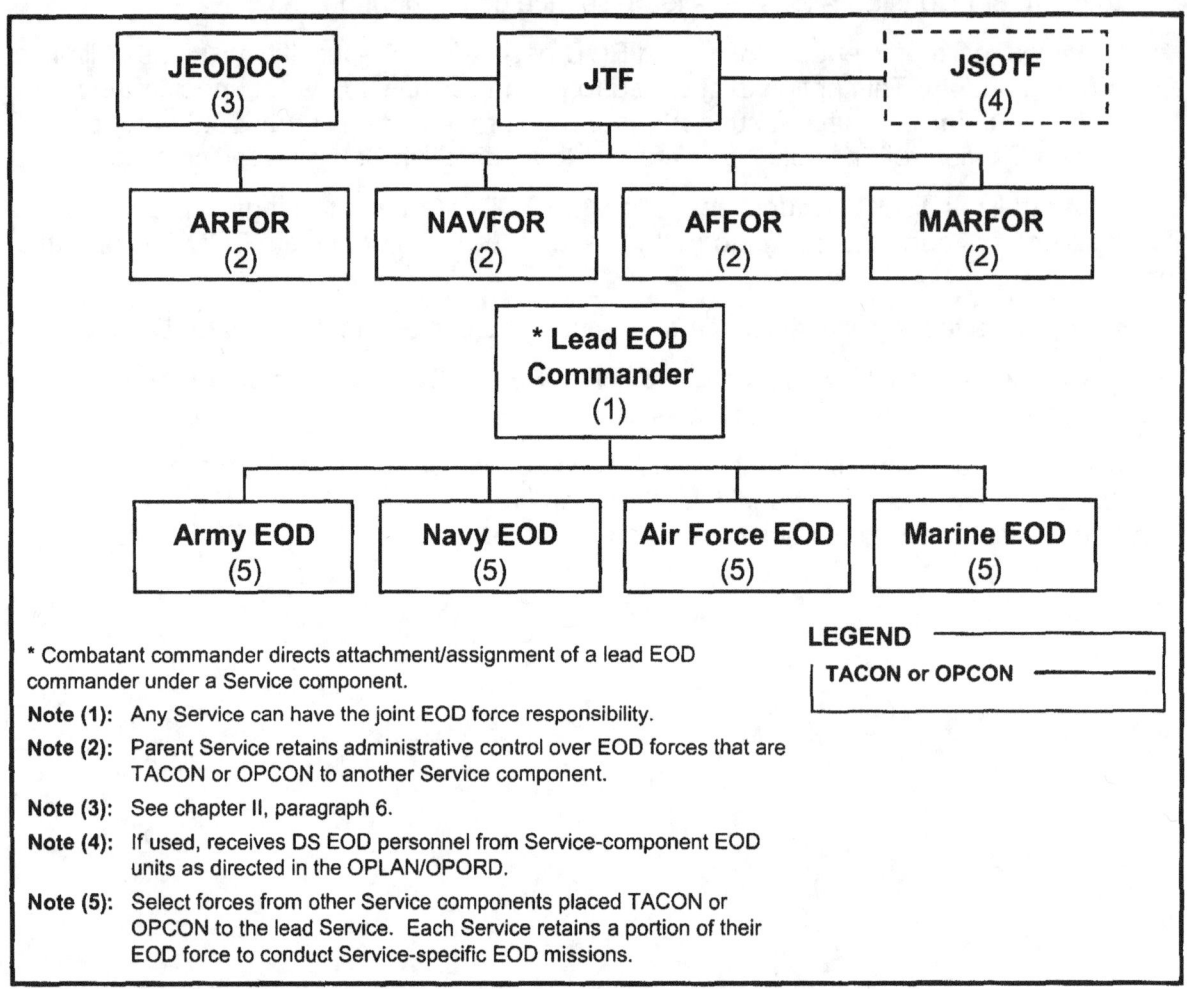

Figure II-2. Lead-Service (with or without TACON/OPCON) Organization

5. Stand-alone or Subordinate EOD JTF Option

a. Utilization. In some operational situations, it may be desirable to form a JTF or subordinate JTF that has a primary EOD function. This JTF would be formed from a major Service EOD unit and would control (via TACON/OPCON for attached units) two or more Service-component EOD organizations and would be jointly staffed. Task organizing EOD forces under a JTF organizational option allows the JFC to focus limited EOD assets where they are needed most and provides an opportunity to optimize EOD mission capabilities. In this option, the JTF would provide the JEODOC function, but will also exercise combatant command (command authority) (COCOM), as opposed to staff management, over any attached EOD units (figure II-3).

b. Formation. The JFC should base the decision to establish an EOD JTF on specific mission needs, while also considering ongoing Service component EOD requirements. The EOD JTF headquarters normally is built around an existing Service-component EOD command, with augmentation from other Service EOD staff personnel. Based on JFC guidance and other considerations, such as an operation plan (OPLAN) and existing agreements, each Service component provides assets to fulfill common EOD support requirements within the JOA. However, even when an EOD JTF is established, Service-unique EOD requirements and selected EOD units may remain under the control of the individual Service components. The combatant and subordinate JFCs should consider the common support requirements needed to allow Service-components the ability to execute their Service-specific requirements. When standing up an EOD JTF, the JFC must ensure that adequate security, administrative, logistical, and medical support is available. See Appendix C for more details on establishing an EOD JTF.

c. Employment Considerations. The EOD JTF option:

(1) Delegates the authority to organize forces to accomplish the EOD mission, based on the JFC's concept of the operation.

(2) Provides the EOD force with unity of effort, centralized planning, and decentralized execution.

(3) Consolidates the capabilities of each Service's EOD force in a joint effort to solve JOA-wide UXO/IED hazards.

(4) Facilitates the JFC control over EOD forces and missions.

(5) Expedites technical intelligence/data acquisition and dissemination to end-users.

(6) Provides a command structure for the integration and control of multinational EOD forces.

(7) May be most appropriate for munitions storage/transportation disasters, or large scale post-hostilities UXO clean-up operations.

(8) Parent Service retains administrative control over EOD forces that are TACON or OPCON to another Service component.

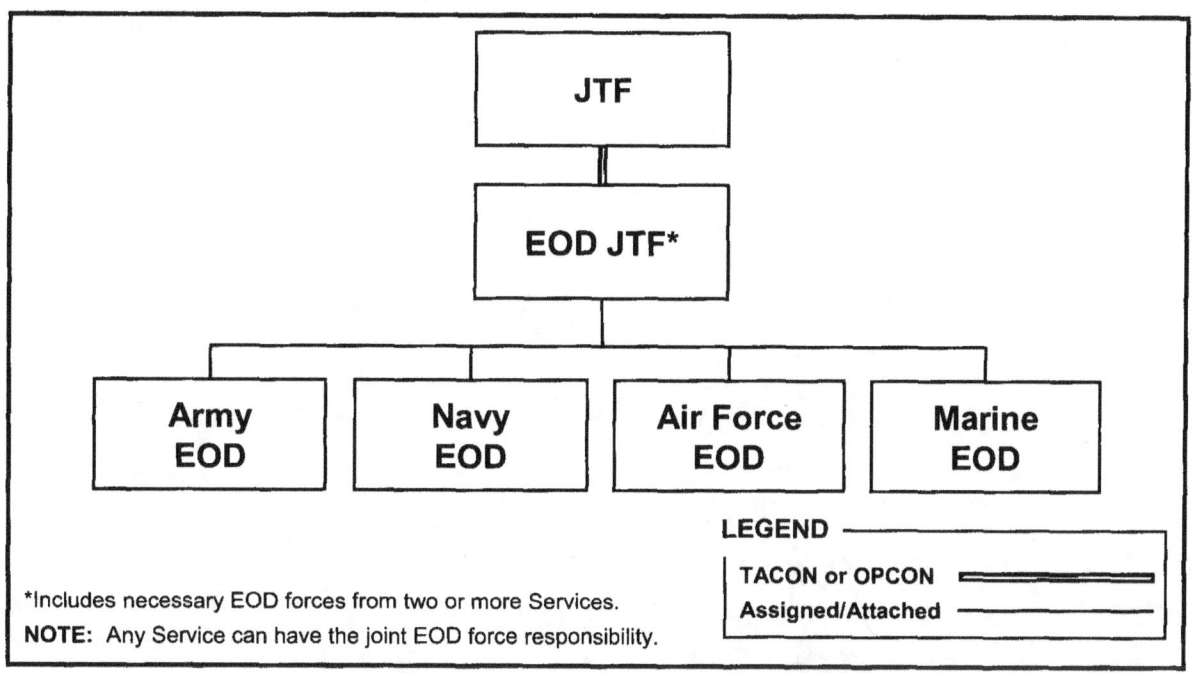

Figure II-3. EOD JTF Organization

6. Information Management and Reporting

a. Information Management (IM). IM refers to the processes a JEODOC uses to obtain, manipulate, direct, and control vital EOD-related information. IM for EOD operations includes all processes involved in the creation, collection and control, dissemination, storage and retrieval, protection, and destruction of critical EOD information. The goal of IM for EOD operations is to provide a timely flow of quality information, enabling the commander of any EOD force to anticipate and understand the consequences of changing conditions. See FM 3-99.4 (FM 101-4)/MCRP 6-23A/NWP 3-13.1.16/AFTTP(I) 3-2.22, *Multi-Service Procedures for Joint Task Force–Information Management*.

    b. Reporting Requirements. See Appendix D, "Standardized EOD Reports."

Chapter III
ARMY EOD OPERATIONS

1. Interservice Responsibilities

Army Regulation (AR) 75-14, Marine Corps Order (MCO) 8027.1D, Chief of Naval Operations Instruction (OPNAVINST) 8027.1G, Air Force Joint Instruction (AFJI) 32-3002, *Interservice Responsibilities and Procedures for Explosive Ordnance Disposal*; and AR 75-15, *Explosive Ordnance Disposal*, defines the Army's responsibilities as the following:

a. To provide EOD support to Army installations/activities and to render safe/dispose of explosive ordnance and IEDs that threatens forces and property in the physical possession of the Army.

b. To provide EOD support in the form of actions and/or advice, when requested from federal agencies or civilian authorities in the interest of public safety. (When available) to provide military support to civil authorities (MSCA)/military assistance to civil authorities (MACA) response to military munitions within the designated area of responsibility.

c. To provide initial response force support to nuclear weapons accidents IAW DOD Directive 3150.8-M, *Nuclear Weapon Accident Response Procedures (NARP)*, 22 February 2005.

2. Mission

The Army EOD mission is to support national security strategy by providing the capability to neutralize hazards from conventional UXO, CBRNE and associated materials, and IED (both explosive and CBRNE), that present a threat to operations, installations, personnel, and/or material. Army EOD forces also may dispose of hazardous foreign or US ammunition, UXO, individual mines, booby-trapped mines, and chemical mines. Breaching and clearance of foreign or US minefields is the primary responsibility of the Army/Marine engineers. EOD provides the Army with a rapidly deployable support package for the elimination of hazards from chemical, biological, radiological, nuclear, and high yield explosives (CBRNE) hazards in any operational environment. The EOD force serves as a combat multiplier by neutralizing UXO/IED that restrict freedom of movement and deny access to or threaten supplies, facilities, and other critical assets. Army EOD forces are equipped, trained, and organized to support tactical land forces across the spectrum of operations (i.e., major combat operations, military operations other than war (MOOTW) including support and stability operations (SASO), MSCA, MACA, and support of combatant commander activities (e.g., humanitarian demining, military to military exchanges, partnership exercises, etc.).

3. Doctrine

a. Force structure rules of allocation (figure III-1).

(1) EOD Group (GP):

(a) Existing rules of allocation are 1 EOD GP per 1-2 Armies, 1 EOD GP with 2-5 EOD battalion (BN), and 1 EOD GP (-) with 1 EOD BN.

(b) Workload rules of allocation are based on mission, enemy, terrain and weather, time, troops available and civil considerations (METT-TC) and military decision making process (MDMP).

- 1 EOD GP or EOD GP (-) per Armies, Corps, or JTF

- 1 EOD GP in support of outside the continental United States (OCONUS) homeland defense

- 1 EOD GP per 3-5 EOD BN

- 1 EOD GP (-) per 1-2 EOD BN

(2) EOD BN:

(a) Existing rules of allocation: 1 EOD BN per 1-3 Corps/Divisions, 1 EOD BN with 3-7 EOD company (CO), and 1 EOD BN (-) with 1-2 EOD CO.

(b) Workload rules of allocation are based on METT-TC and MDMP.

- 1 EOD BN or EOD BN (-) per 1-4 Corps/Divisions

- 1 EOD BN per 3-7 EOD CO

- 1 EOD BN (-) per 1-2 EOD CO

- 1 EOD BN (-) per JTF with 2 or less EOD CO

- 2 EOD BN in support of continental United States (CONUS) homeland defense

- 1 EOD BN per special forces (SF) GP/Ranger BN

- 1-5 EOD BN per Armies

(c) The BN LNO rule of allocation is: 1 per G-3 cell, Corps/Division, and/or maneuver enhancement (ME) chemical, biological, radiological, nuclear and high yield explosives (CBRNE) cell.

(3) EOD CO:

(a) Existing rules of allocation: 1 EOD CO per brigade combat team (BCT), 1/3 EOD CO per SF GP/Ranger BN.

(b) Workload rules of allocation are based on METT-TC and MDMP.

- 1 EOD CO per 1-2 BCT during MOOTW including SASO

- 1 EOD CO per BCT during combat shaping operations

- 1 EOD CO per aerial port of embarkation/aerial port of debarkation/reception, staging, onward movement, and integration area

- 1 EOD CO per 60 sq km

- 11 EOD CO per support to homeland defense CONUS support operations

- 6 EOD CO per Corps/Division

b. C2.

(1) The EOD group provides C2 for all Army EOD assets and operations in the Armies or joint operating AO or as assigned. An EOD group (-) may deploy as the senior C2 element for Army EOD operations in a given Armies operation. EOD battalions remain under the command of their EOD group; depending on the operational situation, they may be placed TACON/OPCON to another unit. When using the TACON/OPCON C2 option, the EOD group retains administrative control (ADCON) of their subordinate battalion(s).

(2) The EOD battalions provide C2, technical intelligence operations, acquisition and management, and limited administrative and logistical support for up to seven EOD companies operating in a JOA. EOD battalions, or battalions (-), may deploy as the senior C2 element for Army EOD operations in a given JTF or Corps/Division operation.

(3) EOD companies remain under the command of the battalion; depending on the operational situation, they may be placed TACON/OPCON to another unit. When using the TACON/OPCON C2 option, the battalion retains ADCON of their subordinate companies. EOD companies provide general support (GS) on an area basis or direct support (DS) to specified BCTs in support of operations. The combatant commander's planning staff tailors EOD forces to support specified operations down to a BCT. Responsibilities of the EOD commander at all levels include:

(a) Recommend policy and distribute EOD assets.

(b) Monitor EOD support missions and establish workload priorities.

(c) Coordinate EOD technical intelligence (TECHINT) operations.

(d) Coordinate GS and DS EOD support.

(e) Provide EOD guidance to force protection procedures to meet existing threat.

(f) Coordinate administrative and logistical support, as required, from the supported command.

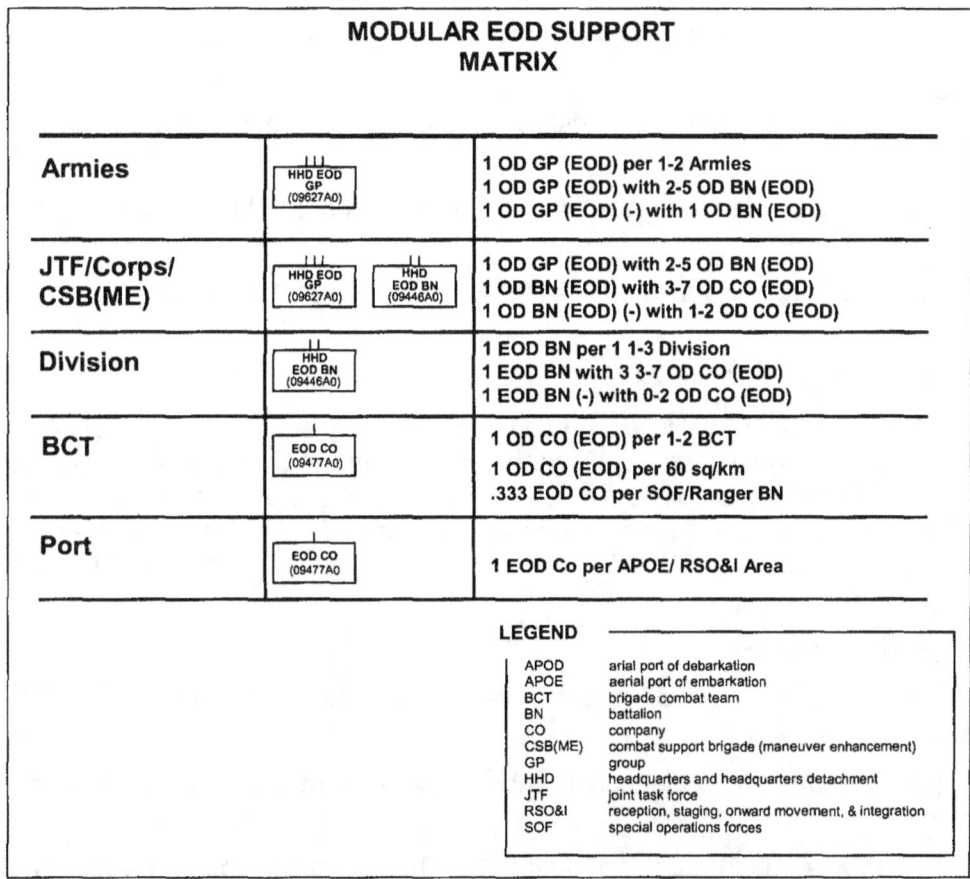

Figure III-1. Modular EOD Support Matrix/Force Structure

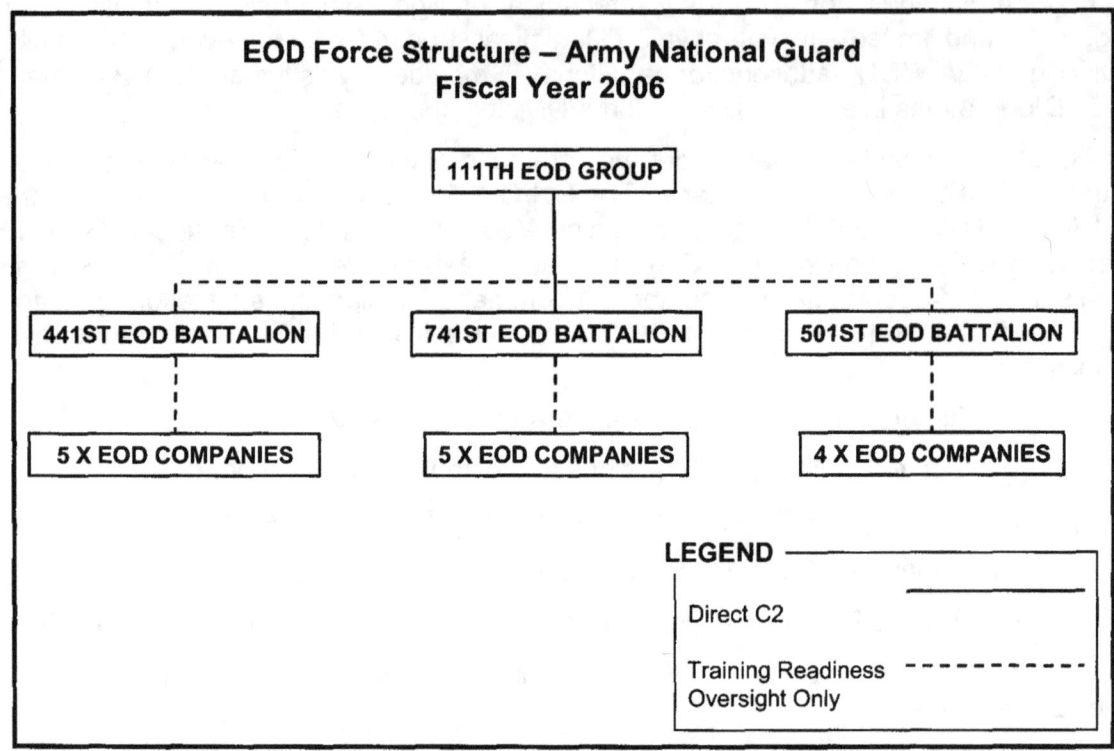

Figure III-2. National Guard EOD Force Structure

(g) Ensure each EOD unit establishes provisions for communications at each level to support EOD operations.

(h) Supplement other theater force protection procedures to meet the existing threat.

(i) Coordinate administrative and logistical support, as required, from the supported command.

c. Armies Strategic Planning.

(1) The Armies G-3 CBRNE EOD cell plans for Army and assigned EOD Armies strategic EOD requirements in support of the geographic combatant commander's campaign plan. The Armies G-3 CBRNE cell accomplishes the planning by using the Joint Operation Planning and Execution System (JOPES) and coordinates the planning effort with the combatant commander's EOD staff officer. The EOD group commander may provide LNOs to the Armies G-3.

(2) The LNO ensures:

(a) Mutual cooperation and understanding between Armies and the EOD group commander.

(b) Coordination on tactical matters to achieve mutual purpose, support, and action.

(c) Precise understanding of stated or implied coordination measures to achieve synchronized results.

d. Corps/Division and Combat Support Brigade (CSB) (ME) Operational Planning.

(1) The Corps/Division G-3 EOD cell provides staff planning for Army EOD operations throughout the Corps/Division AO, and EOD special staff to the Corps/Division commander. Corps/Division G-3 EOD cells are responsible for providing the EOD annex to all respective OPLANs/OPORDs. The CSB (ME) G-3 EOD cell provides staff planning for Army EOD operations in support of CSB (ME) operations and is also responsible for providing the EOD annex to all respective CSB (ME) OPLANs/OPORDs. This imbedded EOD staff capability ensures that EOD forces fully understand and support the maneuver commander's operations and provides for force protection throughout the Corps/Division AO. The EOD BN may provide an LNO to the supported Corps/Division and/or CSB (ME), as determined by METT-TC and JOA task organization.

(2) LNO duties include:

(a) Mutual cooperation and understanding between Corps/Division, CSB (ME), EOD GP and EOD BN commanders.

(b) Coordination on tactical matters to achieve mutual purpose, support, and action.

(c) Precise understanding of stated or implied coordination measures to achieve synchronized results.

e. BCT/CSB (ME) Battalion Operational Planning.

The BCT/CSB (ME) Battalions do not maintain an organizational EOD planning staff capability; rather, they rely upon the supporting EOD company for that capability. The EOD company may provide an operations officer and/or noncommissioned officer (NCO) to the BCT in order to provide appropriate EOD planning and to perform LNO duties, which ensure:

(1) Mutual cooperation and understanding between BCT/ME commanders and staffs and the EOD BN and CO commanders.

(2) Coordination on tactical matters to achieve mutual purpose, support, and action.

(3) Precise understanding of stated or implied coordination measures to achieve synchronized results.

f. Combined Operations Planning.

Combined operations involve the military forces of two or more nations acting together with a common purpose. The Armies or Corps/Division G-3 CBRNE EOD cell considers military doctrine and training, equipment, cultural differences, and language barriers when providing TACON or OPCON of alliance or coalition EOD forces. Lessons learned indicate that few linguists have both the technical expertise and depth of understanding to cross both language and doctrinal boundaries and be fully understood when dealing with UXO and technical EOD procedures. Combined operations require a significant resource commitment to dedicated liaison and linguist teams from alliance or coalition EOD forces.

4. Organizations

The Army assigns EOD organizational assets to specified major command areas (figure III-3). The Army numbers all EOD units for support to specified OPLANs. Major EOD commands and their locations are:

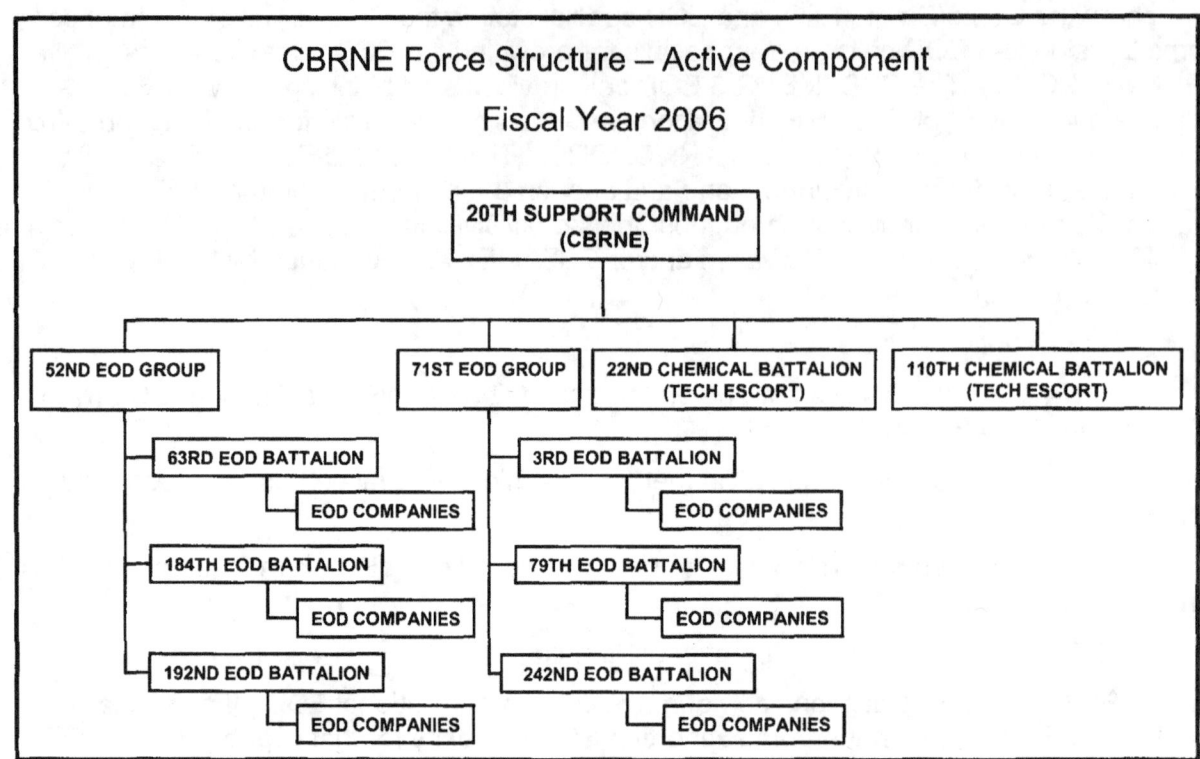

Figure III-3. US Army CBRNE Force Structure

a. US Army Forces Command: 20th Support Command, 2 EOD GPs , 7 EOD BNs, and 44 EOD COs.

b. Seventh US Army, European Command: EOD cell, 191st Ordnance Battalion, and 2 EOD COs.

c. US Army, Pacific Command: EOD control team and 2 EOD COs.

d. Eighth US Army, Republic of Korea: EOD control team and 1 EOD CO.

e. US Army National Guard: 1 EOD GP, 3 EOD BNs, and 14 EOD COs.

5. EOD Company Capabilities

a. The EOD Company—Mission. Each EOD company is authorized 23 soldiers, comprising 20 EOD-qualified technicians, including the commander and first sergeant, and three support soldiers (personnel clerk, mechanic, and supply sergeant). The EOD companies provide support in a DS, GS, and GS-reinforcing relationships throughout the BCT Army force and/or joint force land component commander area of operations. EOD battalion commanders typically task organize their companies in direct support to BCTs. Due to the limited support personnel, EOD companies depend on the supported unit for administrative and logistical support. Additionally, BCTs and/or their subordinate units will be required to provide security for movement of EOD teams in support within the area of operation.

b. The EOD Company—Force Capabilities. The activity of EOD intensifies based upon the operational tempo of the battle and may or may not stabilize as the theater matures. The EOD force within a theater of operations can expect to conduct operations in a myriad of situations and locations. An EOD company can field up to seven EOD teams, consisting of a minimum of one EOD team leader and one EOD team member. Each team can operate for a period up to 72 hours and may conduct 8-10 EOD incidents in a 24-hour period. This is dependent on the mission, enemy, terrain and weather, troops and support available--time available (METT-T). Manpower intensive EOD operations (multiple UXO, CBRNE operations, and ammunition supply point accidents) require several EOD teams at one time to complete the mission. EOD commanders can task organize their teams as necessary to complete the mission.

c.   The EOD Company—Operational Capabilities. Organic to each EOD company are personnel and equipment to identify, mitigate, neutralize, remove, and dispose of conventional or CBRNE explosive hazards. These hazards may arise from domestic or foreign ordnance or IED that degrades the commander's mobility or that threaten personnel, operations, or installations. Many of the capabilities are non-Service specific. To avoid repetition in the Service chapters, Appendix E provides those capabilities that are recurring, non-Service specific EOD requirements. Key Army-specific EOD operational capabilities are:

(1) Improvised Explosive Devices (IED). EOD teams maintain capabilities for remote investigation, identification, and movement of IED, as well as emplacement/operation of disruption tools and disposal methods. Larger IED, such as large vehicle borne IED (VBIED), may require additional EOD support (personnel and equipment) to augment the initial EOD response team.

Note: EOD personnel are the only personnel authorized to respond to requests for IED assistance. EOD personnel are the only personnel equipped, manned, and trained to perform IED render safe procedures (RSP).

---

(2) Force Protection. Army EOD provides the bomb disposal component of the Army's force protection program. In addition to actual response to explosive devices, Army EOD forces can also provide training in UXO/explosives recognition and reporting, bomb threat search procedures and evacuation, site vulnerability assessments, and unit standard operating procedure (SOP) preparation and validation. This training increases the effectiveness of the maneuver commander's force protection program.

(3) Very Important Person Protective Support Activity (VIPPSA). Army EOD is the executive agent (EA) for coordination and tasking of all military EOD support for the Department of State (DOS) and US Secret Service (USSS) for the protection of the President, Vice President, and designated foreign heads of state.

(4) Amnesty Programs. Army EOD units assist in the collection and disposal of hazardous munitions and components as part of the maneuver commander's force protection program, to ensure the continued safety of military personnel.

(5) Stuck Rounds. Each EOD team performs specialized procedures to remove stuck rounds in mortars, artillery, and other weapon systems.

(6) Mortuary Services. Immediate recovery and clearance of deceased persons is a priority of the Services. The presence of UXO being found on or imbedded in deceased persons adversely impacts the recovery of coalition or US personnel. Therefore, Army planners normally involve EOD-qualified leaders in planning and conducting recovery and processing of deceased personnel.

(7) CEA. EOD performs initial munitions assessment of CEA sites, disposal/render safe of munitions that pose an immediate threat, evaluates and identifies CEA for TECHINT and recommends disposition of CEA to capturing unit.

6. Training

a. Required Individual EOD Training. All Army EOD specialists attend the Army-specific material/equipment training (Phase II) at Redstone Arsenal, Alabama. Army EOD personnel also receive continuous technical sustainment training and evaluations at their units of assignment.

b. Specialized Training Opportunities. Select EOD soldiers may also attend specialized training such as technical escort specialist, advanced access and disablement, advanced EOD, and a variety of nuclear and chemical operations courses. A limited number of specially selected EOD soldiers also attend Federal Bureau of Investigation (FBI) civilian EOD training or foreign EOD courses, such as the British Army Engineer IED Disposal and Advanced Manual Techniques Course, the Canadian Military Forces IED Disposal Course, and the French Military Demining School.

c. Combat Training Centers. EOD companies and company elements provide support to maneuver forces (battalions, brigades, and division task force (TF) headquarters) undergoing training at the Joint Readiness Training Center, Louisiana; National Training Center, California; and the Combat Maneuver Training Center, Germany. Specifically, countering UXO hazards with EOD teams prevents needless deaths, injuries, and destruction of the commander's combat power. During reception, staging, onward movement, and integration, supporting EOD teams provide UXO danger awareness and risk management, fratricide prevention, and other safety instruction to JTF personnel.

Chapter IV

MARINE CORPS EOD OPERATIONS

1. Interservice Responsibilities

AR 75-14, MCO 8027.1D, OPNAVINST 8027.1G, AFJI 32-3002, *Interservice Responsibilities and Procedures for Explosive Ordnance Disposal*, defines the Marine Corps responsibilities as follows:

a. USMC EOD forces provide EOD Services on USMC installations, in assigned operational areas of the land mass dispatched for support as the nearest available EOD team, and for explosive ordnance in the physical possession of the Marine Corps.

b. USMC EOD supports SOF in missions requiring tactical delivery and extraction of personnel and equipment by unconventional methods and in missions requiring unconventional small unit tactics, to include direct action (DA) missions.

2. Mission

The USMC EOD mission is to support Marine operating forces, national security strategy, and force protection by locating, accessing, identifying, rendering safe, neutralizing, and disposing of hazards from foreign and domestic, CBRNE, UXO, IEDs, and weapons of mass destruction (WMD) that present a threat to operations, installations, personnel, or materiel.

3. Doctrine

a. Operational Concept. Marine EOD forces provide uniquely/specially/advanced trained personnel to support the Marine air-ground task force (MAGTF) operational concept by eliminating and mitigating all explosive hazards encountered in all spectrums of military operations.

b. C2. Command, control, and coordination of EOD assets falls under the EOD Operations Center (EODOC). The EODOC is located within the MAGTF operations section and staffed with an EOD officer and senior enlisted EOD staff noncommissioned officer (SNCO). The EOD officer is a special staff officer to the MAGTF commander The MAGTF EOD officer tracks all requests for EOD support, plans and prioritizes missions, and provides a liaison capability when conducting joint operations.

c. Operational Planning. For planning, the EOD staff officer (G-3) at Marine Forces, Atlantic (MARFORLANT); Marine Forces, Pacific (MARFORPAC); and Marine Expeditionary Forces (MEFs) advises the commander on all EOD operations. This Marine is responsible to the commander for providing the EOD appendix 13 of annex C for OPLANs/OPORDs to ensure full EOD support in all phases of the operation.

4. Organizations

a. Marine EOD Forces. Marine EOD forces within the MEFs consist of an EOD platoon within the Marine logistics group (MLG) and one EOD team within each Marine wing support squadron (MWSS) of the Marine wing support groups (MWSG) with the Marine aircraft wings (MAW).

(1) The EOD platoon within the MLG is located with the engineer support battalion (ESB). In order to fully leverage the EOD capability across the entire spectrum of MAGTF

operations, particularly during combat and contingency operations, it has been proven over the last 20 years that EOD is best utilized and effective when placed in the MAGTF command element operations section.

(2) An EOD platoon can be task organized in several different ways in order to support Marine operating forces. When an entire MEF is deployed, a typical breakdown of the EOD platoon is depicted below (figure IV-1).

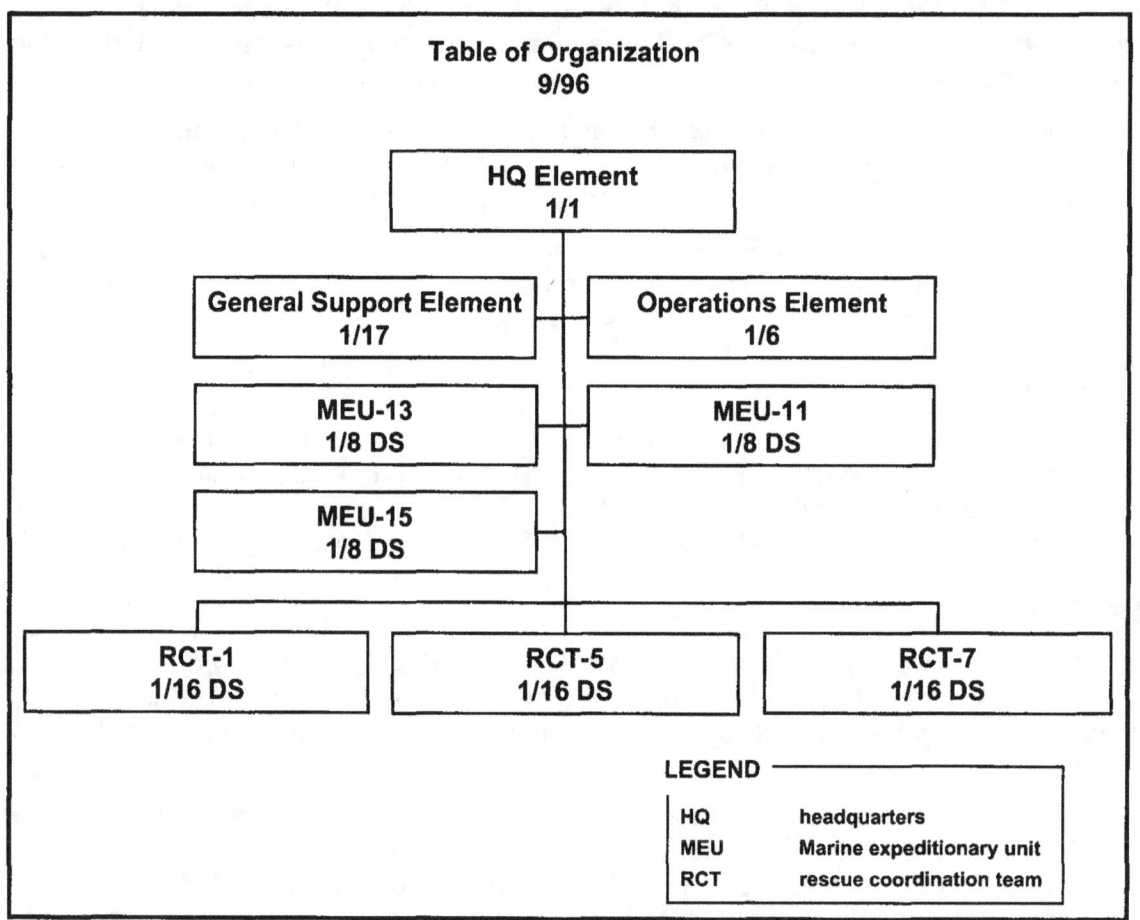

Figure IV-1. USMC EOD Platoon (1 MEF Example)

(3) EOD teams are routinely deployed as MAGTF teams with one officer and eight enlisted personnel. This organizational concept is normally used to support Marine expeditionary unit (special operations capable) [MEU(SOC)] deployments.

(4) The MWSS EOD team consists of one officer and eight enlisted personnel and primarily supports the air combat element, but they are equipped and capable to support all aspects of MAGTF operations. As with the MAGTF, MWSS EOD officers are special staff officers to the MWSS commander (figure IV-2).

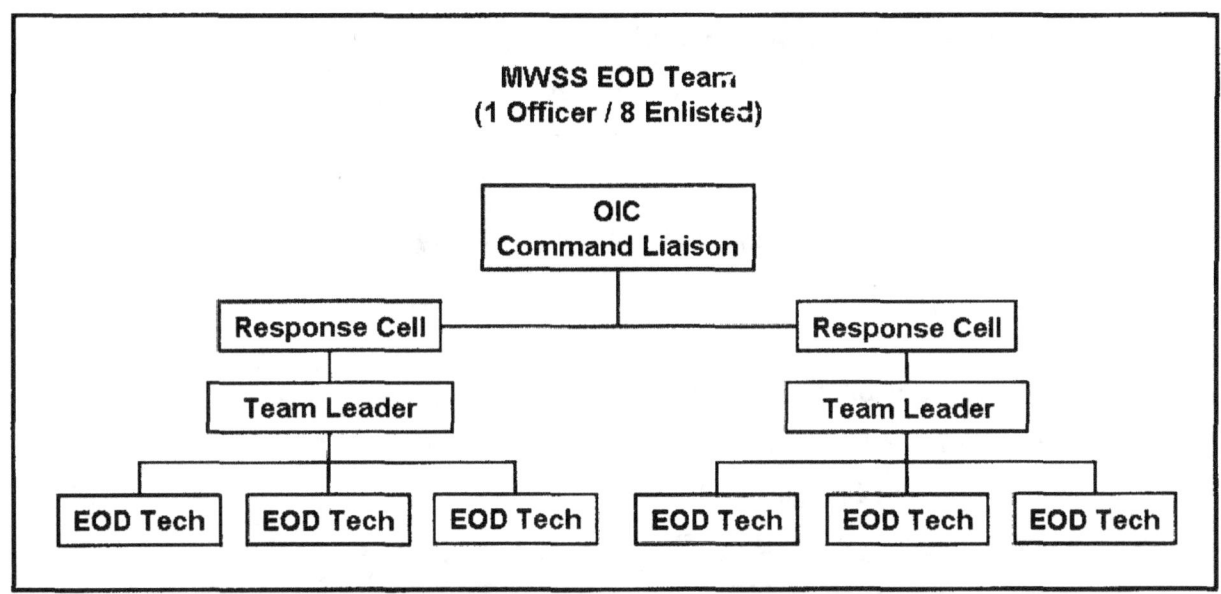

Figure IV-2. USMC EOD Section, Marine Wing Support Squadron

b.   Marine Installation EOD Forces.

Marine Corps Installations East and West (MCIEast, MCIWest). The Marine Corps assigns these EOD teams as a special staff section to the installation commanding officer. The EOD team usually consists of one officer and eight enlisted personnel and provides all support in the conduct of operations and training aboard bases and stations that fall under the MCI commander's area of responsibility. EOD teams remain under the operational and administrative control of installation commanders. These teams support local communities, as well as the installation, with military munition response and IED response in support of homeland defense operations, or if there is not a local bomb squad in the area. In order to maximize the limited EOD assets, most installation EOD teams will stand a combined 24-hour-response duty with the MEF EOD teams aboard that installation.

5. Capabilities

Marine EOD Team Capabilities. In addition to the recurring operations provided in Appendix E, Marine EOD organically possess or can support the following capabilities:

Note: For additional information on Marine EOD capabilities, refer to MCWP 3-17.2, *Explosive Ordnance Disposal*, (MAGTF EOD)

a.   Conventional MAGTF Operations:

   (1) Explosive Threat and Countermunitions Operations.

   (2) Maritime Operations:

      (a) Visit, board, search, and seizure (VBSS), (Surface and Air insertion).

      (b) Small boat raids.

   (3) UXO clearance, RSP, Disposal.

   (4) Aviation Ground Support.

(5) Base Recovery After Attack.

(6) Military operations in urban terrain (MOUT).

(7) CEA.

(8) Tactical Recovery of Aircraft and Personnel.

(9) Stuck Round Removal.

(10) Download/Safing US and Foreign Weapons Systems/Vehicles.

(11) Battlefield Vehicle Recovery Operations.

(12) Stand-off Munitions Disruption.

(13) Ordnance Exploitation/Inerting.

b. Specialized Advanced Skills:

(1) Counterterrorism Driving.

(2) Personnel Security Details (PSD).

(3) Close Quarters Battle (CQB).

(4) Technical Intelligence.

(5) Basic Airborne.

(6) Helicopter Rope Suspension Training.

(7) Advanced Access and Disablement.

(8) Advanced IED Neutralization.

(9) Sensitive Site Exploitation.

c. Weapons of Mass Destruction:

(1) Radiological Emergency Team Operations School.

(2) WMD Command, Control, and Communications (C3).

(3) Radiological Accident C2 (RAC 3).

(4) CBRNE.

d. Specialized Demolitions:

(1) Dynamic Entry.

(2) Target Analysis.

(3) Advanced Explosive Techniques.

e. Anti-Terrorism/Force Protection:

(1) Vulnerability Assessment.

(2) Blast Mitigation.

(3) Post-blast Investigation.

(4) Technical Intelligence.

(5) Crater Analysis.

(6) Large Vehicle Improvised Explosive Devices.

(7) Field Exploitation.

(8) National Security Special Events (NSSE).

6. Training

Team/Individual Qualification Requirements. All EOD personnel, officer/enlisted, must be graduates of the basic course, Naval School Explosive Ordnance Disposal, Eglin Air Force Base, Florida. EOD personnel attend formal advanced training, to include but not limited to, the following schools:

- Joint Nuclear EOD School
- Radiological Emergency Team Operational School
- Dynamic Entry Basic and Advanced (Instructor) Course
- Hazardous Device School
- Advanced IED Disposal (AIEDD) School
- British IED School
- Canadian IED School
- Technical Escort School
- ATF/FBI Post Blast Course
- 40 Hr Hazardous Waste Operators (HAZWOPER) Course
- Confined Space Training
- Radiological Accident C2 (RAC 3) Course
- Nuclear Weapons Orientation Course
- Target Analysis Course
- Proliferation, Terrorism, and Response Course
- Weapons of Mass Destruction, C3 Course
- Basic Airborne School
- Global Antiterrorism Operational Readiness Course (GATOR)
- Advanced Explosives Destruction Techniques (AEDT) – ATF
- Advanced Explosive Investigative Techniques (AEIT) – ATF
- Andros Operations and Maintenance (REMOTECH)
- LVBIED Course – FBI
- Dynamics of International Terrorism
- 18C Course Phase 2

Chapter V
NAVY EOD OPERATIONS

1. Interservice Responsibilities

AR 75-14, MCO 8027.1D, OPNAVINST 8027.1G, AFJI 32-3002, *Interservice Responsibilities and Procedures for Explosive Ordnance Disposal*, defines the Navy responsibilities as follows:

US Navy (USN) EOD provides Services on naval installations; within oceans and contiguous waters, up to the high water mark of harbors, rivers and coastal environments; and emergency response to land mass not specifically assigned as a responsibility of the Army, Marine Corps, or Air Force.

2. Mission

The USN EOD mission is to support national security strategy by providing forces capable of conducting land and underwater detection, identification, render safe, recovery, field evaluation, and disposal of explosive ordnance.

3. Doctrine

The Navy generally categorizes EOD operations into three types: maritime operations, contingency operations, and ordnance intelligence and acquisition.

a. Maritime Operations. The Navy conducts EOD operations to enhance ship survivability, preserve fleet warfighting capabilities, and enable naval, expeditionary, and joint forces to achieve and maintain battlespace dominance through the reduction or elimination of explosive hazards. The Navy assigns EOD forces to carrier strike groups (CSGs), expeditionary strike groups (ESGs), combat expeditionary support (CES), amphibious ready groups (ARGs), Naval Special Warfare Squadrons (NSWRON), and mine countermeasures (MCM) forces. In addition, USN EOD forces are assigned to special contingency operations at sea and ashore (Naval Special Warfare [NSW] and Commanders In-Extremis Force [CIF]), and where continuing EOD requirements exist. Operational commanders employ these forces as necessary to meet theater objectives.

b. Contingency Operations. EOD forces support contingency operations in support of US forces and operations in the interest of national security and safety. Their flexibility and interoperability facilitate partnership with Special Warfare and Marine Corps forces when threats involve conventional ordnance or WMD. From their dedicated fleet and shore assignments, EOD forces support federal and local authorities in the rendering safe and disposal of explosives and explosive devices and assist the USSS in presidential and very important person (VIP) protection. EOD forces also support the Coast Guard in counternarcotics operations and participate in MOOTW such as maritime interdiction, noncombatant evacuation operation (NEO), disaster relief, and security assistance surge operations.

c. Ordnance Intelligence and Acquisition. Navy EOD personnel are qualified divers and can recover ordnance items on land or underwater, make the ordnance explosively safe, and return the item for exploitation. EOD detachments gather immediate preliminary intelligence on threat ordnance in the field. This intelligence is then disseminated to those requiring it in the AO until the detachment or other asset can conduct a more detailed exploitation. Data collected contribute to the development of render safe procedures and support the development of countermeasures, as well as determine the location of enemy stockpiles, types of launch platforms, and tactics.

4. Organizations

The Navy organizes EOD forces to support the geographic combatant commanders. The geographic combatant commander has OPCON of EOD forces through the fleet commanders and numbered fleet commanders. Staff officers within each of these organizations provide C2 and staff planning support for operational EOD activities. See figure V-1 for a depiction of the Atlantic Fleet and European EOD organizational structure and figure V-2 for the EOD organizational structure of the Pacific Fleet.

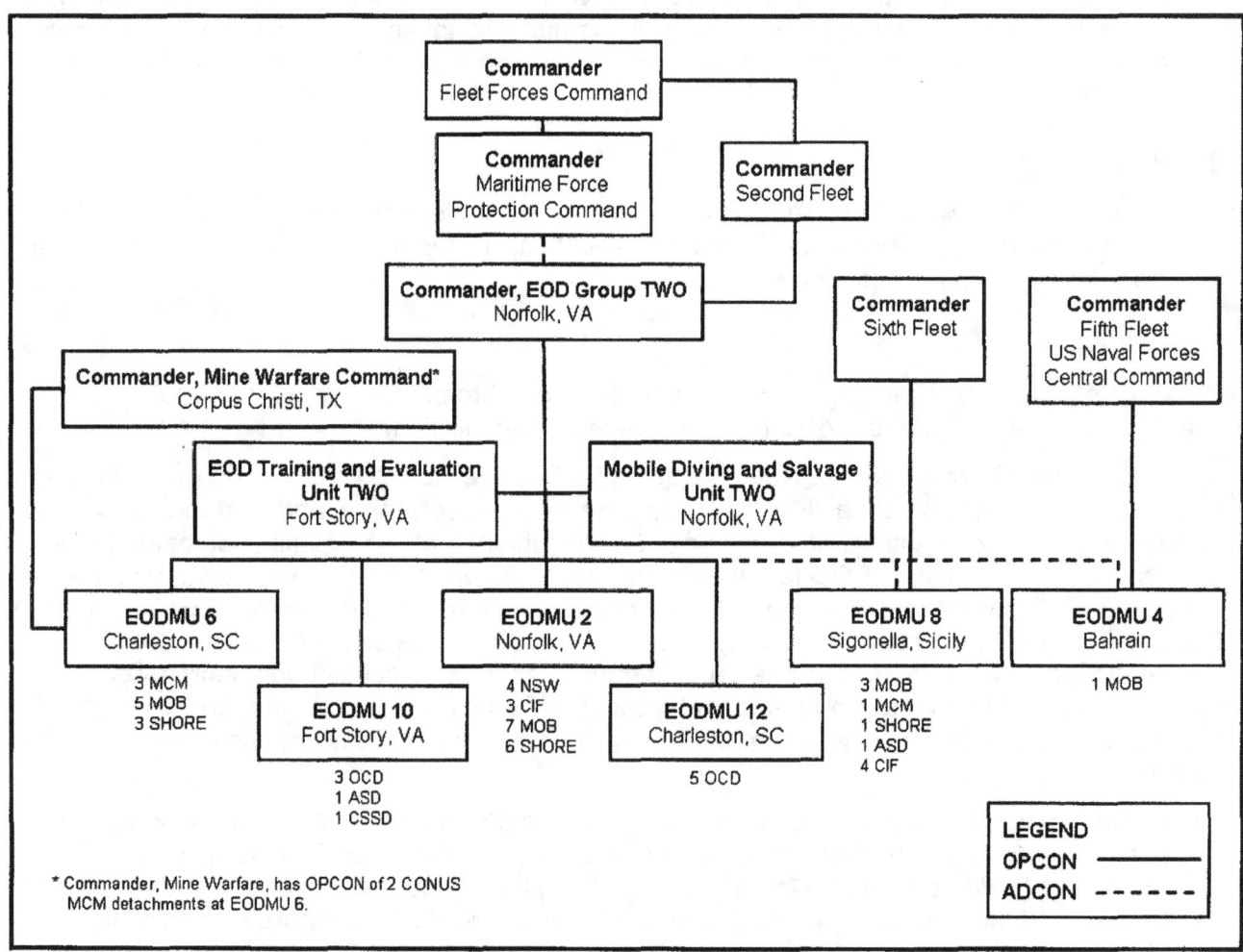

Figure V-1. Atlantic Fleet and European EOD Organization

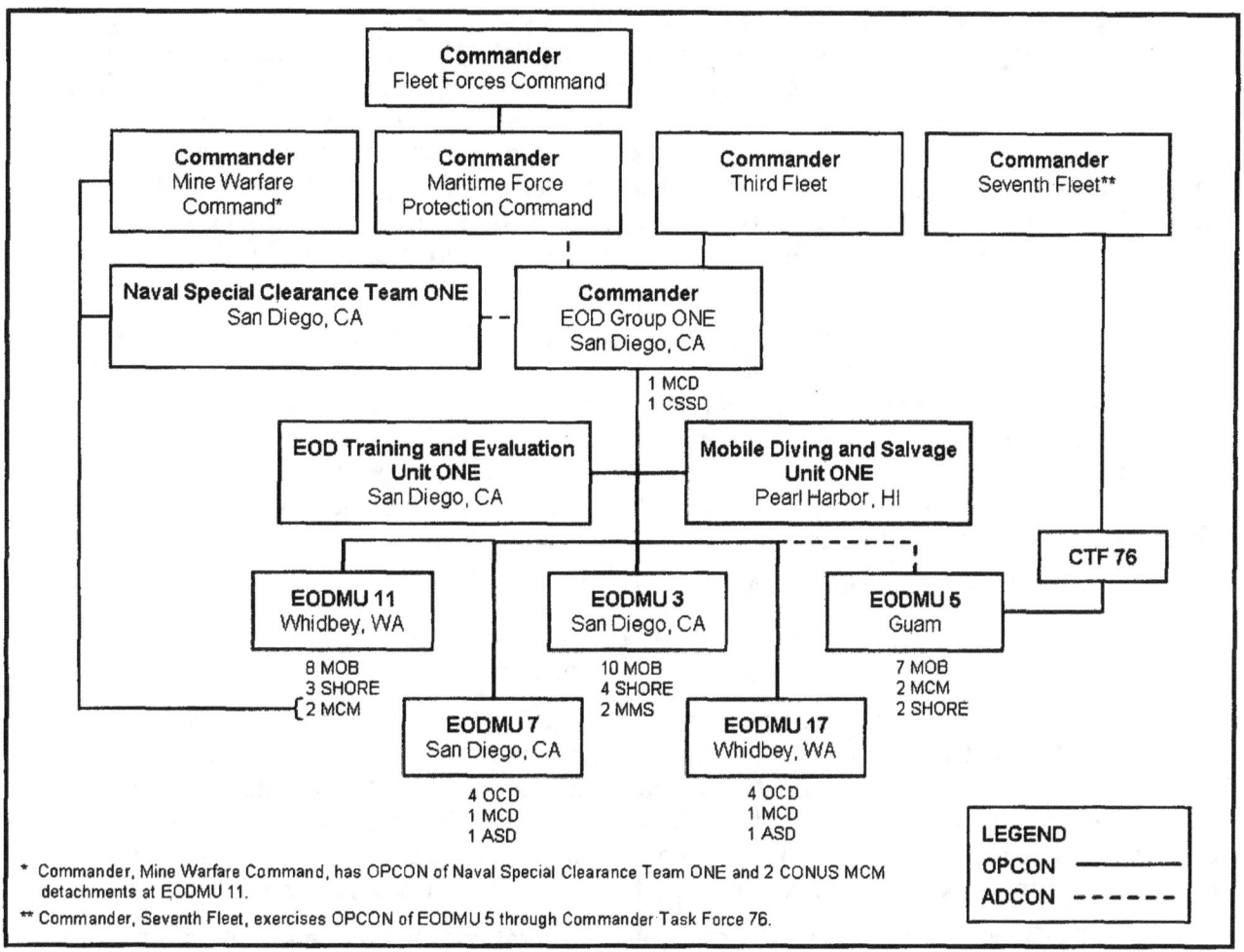

Figure V-2. Pacific Fleet EOD Organization

5. Capabilities

The fundamental operational entity within EOD is the detachment. A detachment is a subordinate element varying from four to eight personnel, capable of independent operations, with assignment to EOD Mobile Units (EODMUs). The best method to describe Navy EOD capabilities is by listing the EOD detachment types. Appendix A identifies specific mission capabilities of each of the major Navy EOD detachments.

a. EOD Mobile (MOB) Detachments. These detachments provide EOD support to CSGs, ESGs, ARGs, NSWRONs, CES/CIF detachments, and theater commanders. The Navy tasks MOB detachments with a variety of contingency operations to include range clearance, USSS support, organic MCM, humanitarian demining operations (HDO), riverine, port security/harbor defense operations, and to augment SOF. The EOD MOB detachment can perform in one of three main configurations—a CSG deployment, an ESG deployment, an ARG deployment, and contingency deployments.

(1) EOD MOB Detachments—CSG Deployments.

(a) Mission. The MOB detachment's mission is to provide an EOD warfare capability to the deployed CSG commander. Navy EOD provides response during flight deck operations involving live, fuzed ordnance and ordnance replenishment evolutions. Also, Navy EOD provides a rapid response to ordnance incidents within the CSG and a forward deployable capability for response to contingencies outside of the CSG. MOB detachments also provide support to maritime interdiction forces, NEO, and other contingency operations in a MOOTW environment and participate in bilateral multinational exercises. MOB detachments can perform a limited amount of minor ships underwater repair tasks. Mobility capabilities include fastrope, rappel, helicopter cast and recovery, specialized personnel insertion/extraction (SPIE) and helicopter deployment of combat rubber raiding craft (CRRC). EOD personnel from these detachments may split into smaller response elements. Normal manning is one officer and seven enlisted personnel.

(b) Assignment. The Navy assigns an EOD MOB detachment to each deploying CSG as a task element. To coordinate C2 of the MOB detachment within the CSG, assignment of the detachment is to the CSG commander. A separate EOD officer and senior enlisted EOD technician is collocated on the CSG commander's platform with the EOD officer performing duties as the task element commander. The EOD officer that performs the task element commander functions also acts as the EOD LNO to plan and direct the employment of detachments/elements as appropriate.

(2) EOD MOB Detachment—ARG Deployment.

(a) Mission. The mission and capabilities are similar to those provided to an ESG with the additional emphasis of supporting amphibious operations afloat and ashore.

(b) Assignment. The Navy assigns an EOD MOB detachment to each ESG or ARG. The ESG or ARG further assigns the detachments to the deployed amphibious squadron/amphibious group. To best coordinate C2 of the MOB detachments within the ARG, the ARG commander has OPCON of the detachment. The ARG commander assigns the detachments as task elements under the amphibious task group. The host ship(s) have TACON of the detachments. Normal manning is one officer and seven enlisted personnel.

(3) EOD MOB Detachments—Contingency Operations Deployment. When the Navy tasks an EOD MOB detachment to perform in a MOOTW environment, the detachment provides EOD personnel to support primary forces engaged in contingency operations including insurgency/counterinsurgency, counterterrorism/antiterrorism, peacekeeping, maritime interdiction, NEO, disaster relief, counterdrug, and security assistance surge operations. Normal manning is one officer and seven enlisted. The EOD MOB detachment performs the following operations in support of contingency operations:

(a) Special Operations Support. EOD forces frequently operate in support of SOF. In Vietnam, Grenada, Panama, and the Persian Gulf, EOD provided direct mission support to dispose of antipersonnel devices, IEDs, and UXO that impeded operations. Any MOB detachment can perform contingency operations in a MOOTW environment such as VBSS or insurgency/counterinsurgency action in support of special operations. Additionally, the Navy permanently assigns a limited number of EOD personnel to the Navy Special Warfare Development Group.

(b) Counternarcotics. The increase in the use of IEDs in the narcotics trade has significantly expanded EOD-force participation in counternarcotics operations. EOD personnel conduct diving and search operations in support of the US Coast Guard, US Treasury, and US Customs Service in counternarcotics and drug interdiction.

(c) EOD Support to Non-DOD and Civilian Organizations. The executive manager for EOD technology and training provides EOD research, technology, and training support to the USSS, the FBI, the Central Intelligence Agency, the US Coast Guard, and the Federal Aviation

Administration. The executive manager provides assistance to other organizations designated by the Secretary of Defense. The Navy provides EOD assistance to render safe and dispose of IEDs, nonmilitary commercial explosives, and similar dangerous articles upon request from federal agencies or civil authorities.

b. Fleet Antiterrorist Security Team (FAST) Company. The commander, EOD Group TWO assigns a detachment from EODMU 2 to support these operations. This detachment augments a Marine company on a rotational basis, as required. Their mission is to support geographical areas experiencing heightened tension resulting from a terrorist threat or regional instability. Normal manning is one officer and seven enlisted personnel.

c. Shore-Based (SHORE) Detachments. The Navy locates EOD SHORE detachments at shore activities that require continuous EOD support. Their mission is to provide an EOD capability to the activity to which they are assigned. EOD support includes general ordnance handling, transportation, storage, disposal and/or safety missions, live-fire training, range clearance, and underwater ordnance testing. The operational commander may deploy the assigned detachment for area or regional response in support of military and civilian incidents or accidents requiring EOD warfare skills. The specific mission determines the actual manning requirements of a SHORE detachment.

d. MCM Detachments.

(1) Mission. EOD MCM detachments are part of the dedicated mine warfare force and are specialized detachments that locate, identify, neutralize, recover, exploit, and dispose of sea mines. These detachments provide the MCM commander with an underwater capability. They normally conduct integrated operations with surface mine countermeasures (SMCM) and airborne mine countermeasures (AMCM) units and are also capable of limited independent operations. MCM detachments maintain basic warfighting capabilities equivalent to those of MOB detachments in the conventional ordnance and IED threat response areas. MCM detachments have special low-influence signature (magnetic and acoustic) equipment and capabilities. The detachments are also responsible for recovering new mine types and subsequently conducting tactical field exploitation of the recovered mines, a mission critical to the effectiveness of all MCM operations. Normal manning is one officer and seven enlisted personnel.

(2) Assignment. The Navy often assigns MCM detachments under OPCON of an MCM squadron commander. Each deploying MCM squadron normally consists of a command/support ship, an AMCM unit, an SMCM unit, and an underwater mine countermeasures (UMCM) unit. The UMCM command task unit is normally the commanding officer of EODMU THREE or EODMU SIX (or their designated representative). The UMCM task unit normally consists of two or more MCM detachments and other EOD detachments as assigned. The EOD command task unit is the MCM squadron commander's primary advisor for planning and executing safe and efficient UMCM operations.

e. Marine Mammal System (MMS) Detachments. MMS detachments provide an enhanced capability to detect, identify, mark, render safe, recover, and neutralize objects within the water column as well as those that have become buried under the ocean's floor. All MMS detachments are mobile systems that can rapidly deploy to most areas of the world on short notice utilizing fixed-wing aircraft, helicopters, trucks, boats, amphibious ship well decks, or command ship. The Navy's current marine mammal program has one fleet operational site and one fleet support facility, both located in San Diego, California. These highly mobile, reliable, and effective systems provide a trained, contingency response capability in the following mission areas:

(1) Mark (MK) 4 Module (MOD) 0 MMS (Close-Tethered, Deep-Moored Mine hunting, and Neutralization System). This MMS detachment is an underwater surveillance and detection system which employs dolphins for object location, marking, and recovery with the mission of detecting and neutralizing close-tethered, deep-moored mines. The system provides an effective tool for port break-in and breakout missions as well as MCM operations at naval choke points, anchorages, along known/suspected mine routes (Q-routes) and in vital sea lanes. Normal manning is one officer and 18 enlisted personnel.

(2) MK 5 MOD 1 MMS (Pingered Object Recovery System). This MMS detachment is a recovery system that uses sea lions to locate and attach recovery hardware to mines and test ordnance with acoustic pingers attached to them. Normal manning is one officer and 13 enlisted.

(3) MK 6 MOD 1 MMS (Swimmer Detection and Defense System). This MMS detachment is a waterside security system that uses dolphins to protect harbors, anchorages, and individual assets against unauthorized swimmers, divers, and swimmer delivery vehicles. It can be employed in MOOTW, antiterrorist, or traditional port and anchorage scenarios. Normal manning is one officer and 20 enlisted personnel.

(4) MK 7 MOD 1 MMS (Bottom and Buried Minehunting and Neutralization System). This MMS detachment is a mine detection, location, and neutralization system that uses dolphins to detect and neutralize proud mines (mines on the ocean floor) and mines buried under the ocean bottom. Normal manning is one officer and 25 enlisted personnel.

f.   Area Search Detachments (ASDs).

(1) ASD Underwater Systems. ASDs detect and locate underwater ordnance on the ocean bottom by using side-scan sonar, towing hardware/cables, and precise navigation systems. The sonar and associated equipment are portable and have a relatively small logistic footprint for employment on an ASD craft of opportunity. Although ASDs are flexible and mobile, their effectiveness is largely limited to areas of smooth and hard bottoms. Buried mines, certain mine shapes, cluttered and uneven bottoms, and moored mines reduce the effectiveness of ASDs for MCM operations. Normal manning is one officer and four enlisted personnel.

(2) ASD Deployment and Mission. ASDs deploy from EODMUs or mobile diving and salvage units (MDSU) to perform underwater search operations to locate salvageable objects such as aircraft or large debris to be removed from sea lanes. These operations occur during channel conditioning operations and support the conduct of port breakouts and overseas port facility recovery operations. ASDs also use their assets to reacquire mine-like objects previously detected by other MCM assets and systems. EOD ASDs provide a limited mine-detection capability when a low-profile presence or very rapid response is desired, and the increased risk to the host platform is acceptable. ASDs can pass position data and mark contacts for prosecution by EOD MCM detachments and can operate in both salt and fresh water.

g.   Fly-Away Recompression Chamber Detachment. This detachment provides emergency hyperbaric recompression treatment for personnel who experience diving-related injuries when a local chamber is not available. The fly-away recompression chamber can locate on an MCM command/support ship, a craft of opportunity, or ashore. Normal manning is three divers, one diving medical technician, and one diving medical officer.

h.   Naval Special Clearance Team.

(1) Very shallow water (VSW) Mission. The mission of the VSW MCM detachment is to provide a small cadre of specially trained and equipped forces to conduct low-visibility mine exploration and reconnaissance operations in the VSW zone (10-40 feet). Primary functional

areas include: confirming the presence or absence of mines in selected VSW areas, re-acquiring and identifying previously detected mine-like contacts in the VSW zone, and providing the tactical commander with data from VSW zone exploratory and reconnaissance missions to predict mine density. Supporting functional areas involves diving and demolition operations. VSW MCM forces must apply primary and supporting functional areas described above by employing specific VSW MCM-unique equipment, procedures, and tactics to counter the VSW mine threat.

(2) VSW Assignment and Operations. VSW serves as a component of the Navy's dedicated MCM forces under OPCON of commander, mine warfare command, and ADCON of commander, EOD Group ONE. The detachment participates in fleet MCM exercises and conducts regular fleet training to develop and refine VSW MCM tactics. Additionally, they serve as a warfighting laboratory for assessing the performance of new technologies to address MCM reconnaissance in the VSW zone. In the event of contingency operations, the VSW detachment maintains a 48-hour fly-away capability for short-notice embarkation in advance force platforms assigned under the commander, amphibious task force (CATF) and the MCM commander when the MCM commander is assigned under the CATF. The VSW detachment can mobilize with specialized equipment and tactics to enhance advance force and pre-assault MCM capabilities in support of amphibious operations in a mined environment. Current manning totals 70 personnel—seven officers and 46 enlisted personnel from the Navy and one officer and 16 enlisted from the Marine Corps.

i.   EOD Command, Control, Communications, Computers, and Intelligence (C4I) Cell. Individual EOD and MDSU detachments are currently assigned in support of various plans/contingency plans. As multiple detachments deploy, EOD forces may deploy as a single unit under the control of their commanding officer. Operations may require employment of EOD detachments simultaneously in close proximity or rapidly dispersed to remote areas for independent operations. Accordingly, an EOD C4I capability is required to assist in eliminating fratricide and providing force identification and logistical support. Experience during Operation DESERT STORM, numerous exercises, and MOOTW have routinely demonstrated that an EOD C4I cell provides effective C4I, logistics, and medical support to the deployed EOD and MDSU detachments. The deployed EOD C4I cell also facilitates organic support capabilities to sustain operations for long periods. Normal manning is two officers and seven enlisted personnel.

j.   Naval Reserve Force (NRF) Detachments. NRF detachments are maintained within the NRF EODMUs. They provide contributory support during peacetime and crisis response during MOOTW, major regional conflicts, and contingency operations. NRF detachments are comprised of selected reserve personnel, who maintain capabilities in diving, basic demolition, ordnance location, identification, and disposal. There are three types of NRF detachments: ordnance clearance detachments (OCDs), mobile communications detachments (MCDs), and ASDs.

(1) OCDs provide diving and demolition support, perform manpower-intensive EOD-related tasks that enable EOD detachments to be available for more technical procedures, and act as force multipliers when integrated with regular forces. OCDs can locate, identify, and destroy conventional ordnance, but they do not perform render-safe or exploitation procedures. OCDs conduct routine hull/pier/underwater searches, locate/identify/destroy underwater ordnance in support of MCM port clearance operations, and provide contributory support in the areas of search-and-rescue retrograde ordnance/explosives disposal and range clearance operations. For MCM operations, OCDs work in conjunction with other MCM assets to provide additional identification and neutralization capabilities. Normal manning is one officer and six enlisted personnel.

(2) MCDs provide a deployable field communications cell for integrated command post tactical and strategic communications in support of EOD forces in the field. Capabilities include Global Command and Control System, secure voice, data, and imagery radio-frequency communications in the high frequency, ultrahigh frequency line of sight, satellite communications, and very high frequency spectrum. Normal manning is one officer and four enlisted personnel.

(3) ASDs were described in paragraph 5f above.

k. MDSUs. In addition to assigned EOD units, EOD Group ONE and EOD Group TWO have ADCON over MDSU ONE and MDSU TWO, respectively. MDSUs provide mission-capable active and naval reserve detachments to perform diving, salvage/recovery, and underwater ship-repair operations in ports or harbors. They can operate from ports, US Navy and Military Sealift Command vessels, or commercial contract salvage or repair vessels. In addition, the MDSU detachments provide limited self-defense. Each MDSU has mobile diving and salvage detachments and fleet maintenance diving detachments. These detachments can simultaneously deploy to different areas of the world in support of their assigned mission areas.

6. Training

a. Diver Training. Navy EOD Candidates attend and must complete EOD diver training, conducted at the Naval Diving and Salvage Training Center, Panama City, FL prior to attending EOD Technician School. Students are taught self-contained underwater breathing apparatus (SCUBA) and MK16 mixed gas (UBA).

b. Tactical Insertion/Extraction. Navy EOD Technicians perform tactical insertion and extraction of personnel and equipment by unconventional methods (e.g. SPIE, rappel, fastrope, casting, CRRC) in areas that cannot be accessed/reached by conventional means. Select mobile and shore detachments maintain land and water parachute insertion capabilities (PIC) for emergent worldwide support. Tactical Insertion/Extraction training is taught at EODTEU ONE in San Diego, CA immediately following EOD school.

c. EOD Training and Evaluation Units (EODTEUs). EODTEUs provide readiness improvement training to EOD detachment personnel preparing for operational deployments. Detachments are guided through advanced TTP classroom training, followed by advanced practical exercises in all core mission areas. EODTEUs provide similar training to shore and naval reserve detachment personnel. Additionally, training units provide specialized, high-risk supervisory training for demolition/burn range operations, SPIE/rappel/fast rope operations, SCUBA/MK-16 underwater breathing apparatus operations and field communications procedures. EODTEUs also conduct field evaluation of new and experimental EOD tools and equipment prior to distribution to operational units.

Chapter VI
AIR FORCE EOD OPERATIONS

1. Interservice Responsibilities

AR 75-14, MCO 8027.1D, OPNAVINST 8027.1G, AFJI 32-3002, *Interservice Responsibilities and Procedures for Explosive Ordnance Disposal*, defines the Air Force EOD responsibilities as follows:

a. Air Force EOD teams furnish their services on Air Force installations, dispersal bases (which include DOD installations from which air reserve component forces operate), in assigned operational areas, or for the disposal of explosive ordnance in the physical possession of the Air Force.

b. When requested by other Services, federal agencies, or civil authorities, Air Force EOD teams respond to any incident site to prevent or limit damage and injury.

c. They provide Initial Response Force (IRF) and Response Task Force (RTF) support to nuclear weapons accidents IAW DOD Directive 3150.8-M.

2. Mission

The Air Force EOD mission is to protect people, facilities, and resources from the damaging effects of UXO, hazardous components, and devices. The EOD personnel locate, identify, disarm, neutralize, recover, and dispose of hazardous explosives, CBRNE, and incendiary items. They also neutralize criminal and terrorist bombs when requested or directed by proper authority, clear areas of explosives-related contamination, and dispose of unserviceable and outdated munitions. The EOD force supports the USSS and the DOS in their protection of the President, Vice President, foreign dignitaries, and VIPs. EOD forces train other Air Force personnel on ordnance recognition, hazards, and precautions and provide EOD support to the global engagement mission.

3. Doctrine

a. Concept. The Air Force organizes EOD force packages into unit type codes (UTCs) to provide flexible structures to support contingency missions. The Air Force designs these packages to meet specific manning and equipment requirements based on the mission and threat. Planners can combine the UTCs in building-block fashion to provide coverage for location-specific missions.

b. C2. In peacetime, Air Force assigns EOD units to an Air Force wing under the base civil engineer (BCE) and further assigns the wings to the major commands (MAJCOMs) through the Numbered Air Forces. During deployed operations, Air Force assigns EOD units under the deployed BCE (when one is assigned). If no BCE is assigned, EOD units normally work for the deployed wing/unit commander. At the wing level during increased threat conditions, the wing establishes a survival recovery center (SRC) for wing C2. The senior EOD representative performs duties at the SRC to control all EOD operations at the deployed location.

c. Operational Planning. The Air Force provides basic UTC packages for planners to develop capabilities at deployed locations. These UTCs form capabilities to respond to the various threat levels. This building-block approach allows the maximum flexibility in EOD force employment. Air Force EOD UTCs are:

(1) 4F9X1-EN EOD Core Equipment Set. This UTC comprises EOD specialized equipment, vehicles, and explosives required in the initial EOD support of major combat, contingency, and homeland defense operations. The equipment and explosives are loaded on vehicles to provide a roll-on roll-off capability to protect personnel and resources from the effects of explosive hazards, munitions accidents, and UXO to include IED. It provides limited capability to assess and mitigate chemical, biological, radiological, nuclear and explosive threats. Task UTC UFM3X (EOD M1116 UA-HMMWV), UFMXX (EOD M1097 HMMWV) and UFMTA (HIGH MOBILITY TRAILER). This UTC contains sensitive/mission-critical EOD equipment requiring an EOD escort, 4FPXC or 4FPXD, during transport. Expeditionary combat support is required.

(2) 4F9X3-EN EOD Base Sustainment Equipment. This UTC comprises EOD specialized equipment and explosives required to provide base sustainment in the support of major combat, contingency, and homeland defense operations where the EOD core (4F9X1) UTCs already exists or is scheduled for deployment. It protects personnel and resources from the effects of explosive hazards, munitions accidents, and UXO to include IED. It provides limited capability to assess, access, disrupt, neutralize or render safe chemical, biological, radiological, nuclear and explosive threats. This UTC contains sensitive/mission-critical EOD equipment requiring an EOD escort, 4FPXC or 4FPXD, during transport. Expeditionary combat support is required.

(3) 4F9X4-EN EOD Installation Equipment. This is an equipment only UTC. This base support equipment UTC is required to provide 24-hour emergency and routine EOD support at home station installations. This UTC supports homeland defense and force protection operations when paired with companion UTC 4FPXB (1), 4FPXC (1), 4FPXD (2), and 4FPXE (1). It provides capabilities to detect, defeat, and recover from hazardous munitions incidents/accidents on and off installations for military munitions and terrorist devices including WMD. This UTC contains all necessary specialized EOD equipment to support operations identified above to include robotics, vehicles, and explosives. This UTC is intended for generation only and is not intended for deployment. This is an equipment only UTC.

(4) 4F9X5-EN EOD Explosive Storage Magazine. This UTC is a deployable explosive storage magazine set used to store EOD demolition packages required in the support of major combat, contingency, and homeland defense operations. The magazine is designed to significantly reduce explosive hazard class and quantity distance requirements. It is used for temporary explosive storage during initial contingency operations until siting of permanent explosive storage areas are established. The magazines are employed during homeland defense operations to support EOD emergency responses. This UTC includes an Air Force standard security system required for storage of high risk munitions.

(5) 4F9X7-EN EOD Large Robotic System. This UTC is one EOD all-purpose remote transport system complete with associated equipment. This UTC is used to provide EOD teams a remote vehicle for large area clearance, base recovery, render safe procedure and/or WMD operations which involve UXO, IED, or large vehicle IED. This UTC can be employed in the support of major combat, contingency, and homeland defense operations. This UTC contains sensitive/mission-critical EOD equipment requiring an EOD escort, 4FPXC or 4FPXD, during transport.

(6) 4F9XA-EN EOD Officer. An EOD officer is required in the support of major combat, contingency, and homeland defense operations where EOD personnel and equipment already exist or are scheduled for deployment. The EOD officer Independently provides forward command functional management. 4FPXA may be linked with 4FPXB to form an EOD management team. Personnel will deploy with personal protective clothing and GUU-5 (M-4)

and M-9 weapons with ammunition. ECS required. Substitution in accordance with AFI 10-210, *Prime Base Engineer Emergency Force (BEEF) Program*, 1 October 2004. 032E4 must be an EOD qualified officer presently filling an authorized EOD position and/or validated by MAJCOM EOD functional manager.

(7) 4F9XB-EN EOD Senior NCO Management. This UTC is the EOD management force that is required in the support of major combat, contingency, and homeland defense operations where EOD personnel and equipment already exist or are scheduled for deployment. It independently provides forward command functional management. 4FPXB may be linked with 4FPXA to form an EOD management team. Personnel will deploy with personal protective clothing and GUU-5 (M-4) and M-9 weapons with ammunition. ECS is required. Substitution of 3E800 with 3E891 is authorized. For Air Reserve Component (ARC) forces: where two 4FPXB UTCs are postured, the second UTC wartime record will flow as a 3E891-SMSGT.

(8) 4F9XC-EN EOD Team Leadership. EOD team leadership is required in the support of major combat, contingency, and homeland defense operations. This UTC is linked with UTC 4F9X1 or can augment existing requirements. Personnel will deploy with personal protective clothing and M-4 and M-9 weapons with ammunition. MSGT 3E871 is required; no substitution is authorized. Substitution of 7 LVL AFSC allowed using only 3E8XX, two skill levels up or one skill level down; no other substitutions authorized.

(9) 4F9XD-EN EOD Craftsman Team. The EOD craftsman team is required in the support of major combat, contingency, and homeland defense operations. This UTC is linked with UTC 4F9X1, 4F9X3, or can augment existing requirements. Personnel will deploy with personal protective clothing and M-4 and M-9 weapons with ammunition. 3E871 is required; no substitution authorized. Substitution of 5 LVL AFSC allowed using only 3E8XX, two skill levels up or one skill level down.

(10) 4F9XE-EN EOD Journeyman Team. The EOD journeyman team is required in the support of major combat, contingency, and homeland defense operations. This UTC is linked with UTC 4F9X1, 4F9X3, or can augment existing requirements. Personnel will deploy with personal protective clothing and M-4 and M-9 weapons with ammunition. Substitution of only one 5 LVL AFSC allowed using only 3E8XX, two skill levels up or one skill level down. No other substitutions authorized.

4. Organizations

During peacetime, the Air Force assigns EOD flights to the civil engineer (CE) organization within the MAJCOMs. They are responsible for peacetime support of the command mission and posturing deployable force packages (figure VI-1). In wartime, the EOD force deploys to support the geographic combatant commanders (figure VI-2).

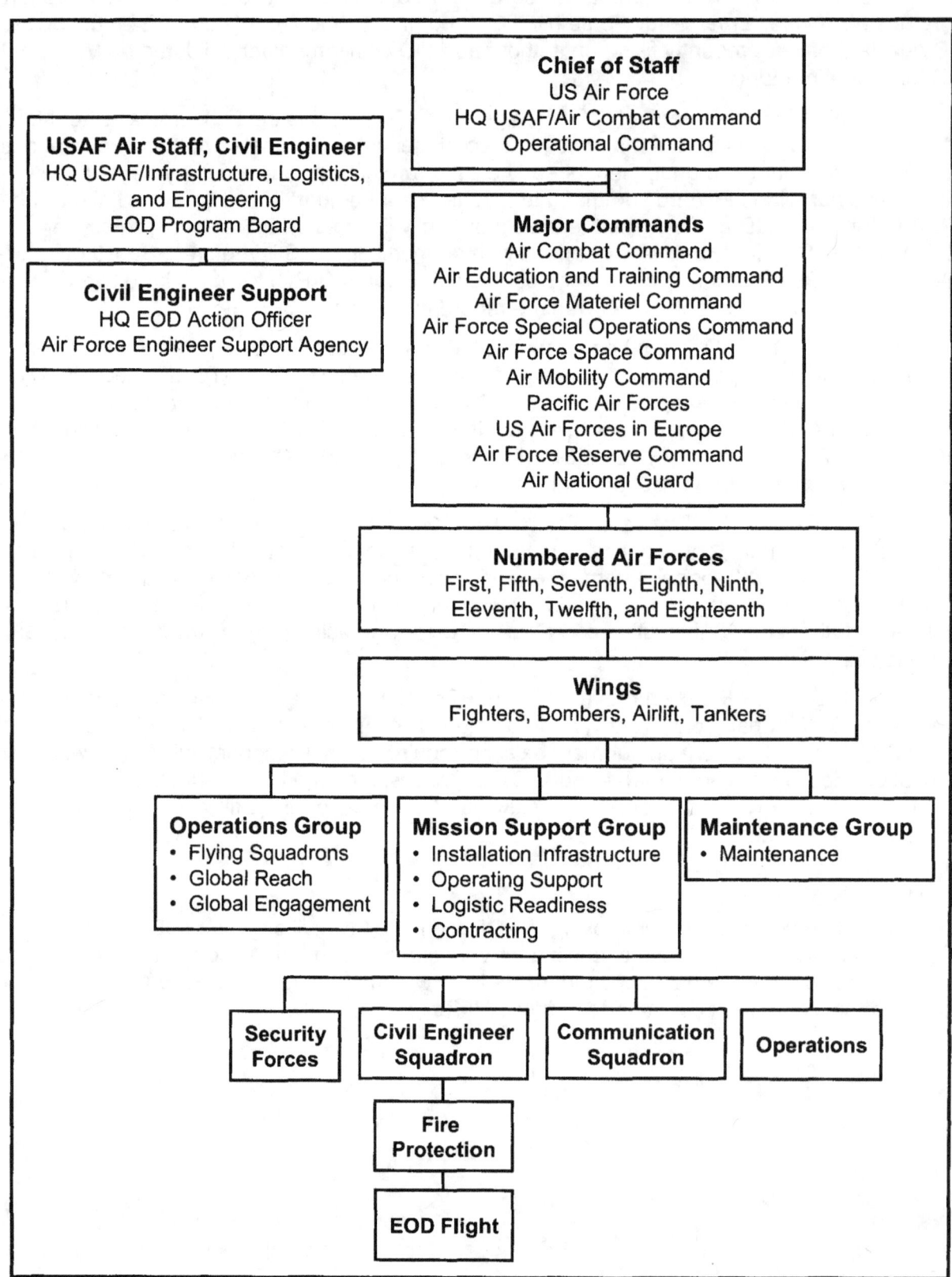

Figure VI-1. Air Force Peacetime EOD Organization

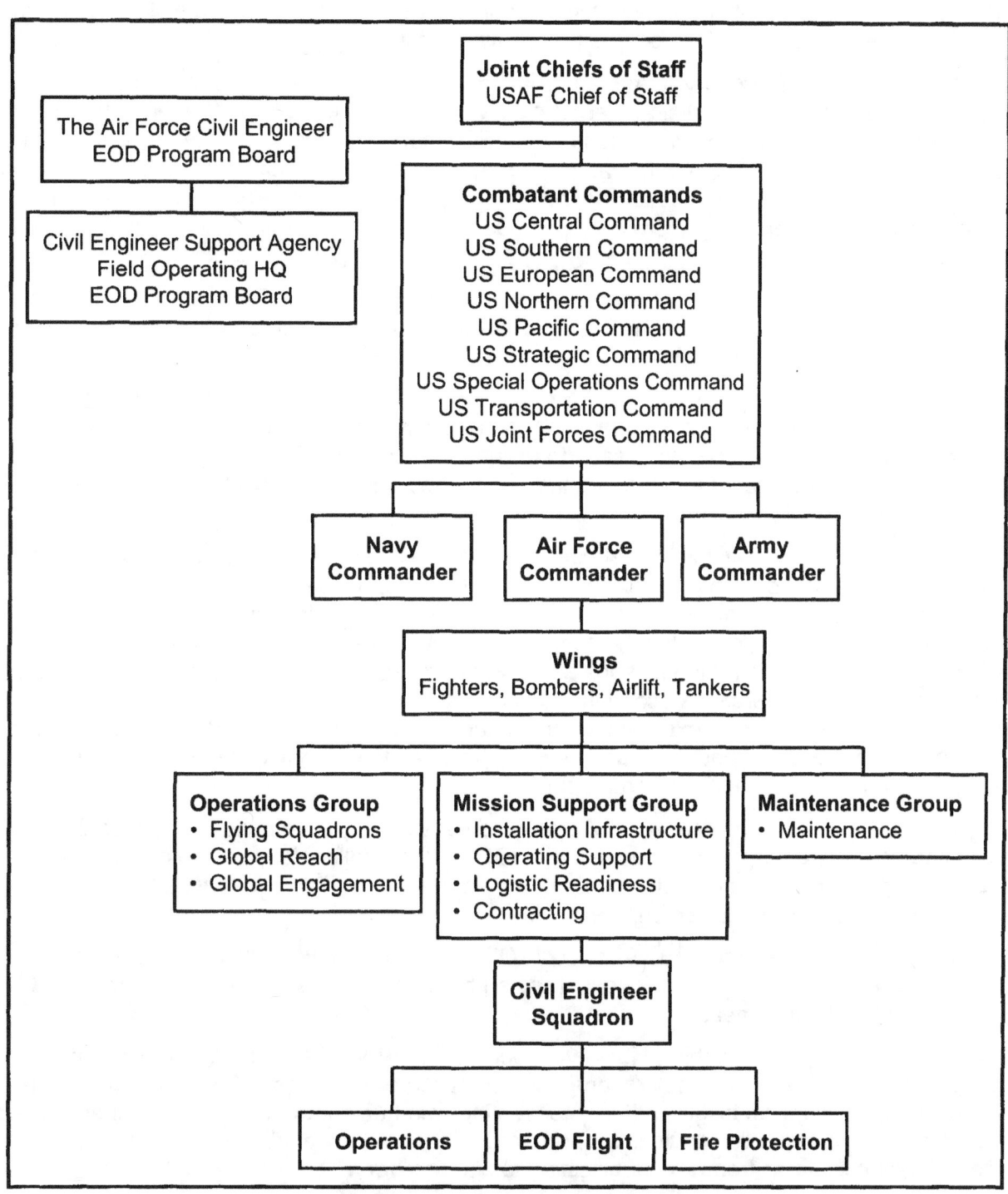

Figure VI-2. Air Force Wartime EOD Organization

5. Capabilities

a. General. The minimum EOD team size for incident responses is two qualified operators employing remote procedures whenever possible. If available, a third EOD-qualified supervisor provides on-scene safety, supervision, and command advice.

b. Capabilities. In addition to the recurring, non-Service-specific EOD capabilities at appendix E, the Air Force EOD force has the following responsibilities:

(1) Launch and Recovery of Aircraft. Air Force EOD teams directly support sortie generation. They respond to airfield emergencies according to peacetime requirements of unreleased or unsafe ordnances/munitions, other EOD safety issues, resource protection, and situations requiring sound judgment. Wartime operations involving aircraft differ from peacetime operations primarily from an increased operations tempo and requirement for aircraft battle damage assessments ensuring there are no UXOs.

(2) Force Protection. To provide a secure environment, Air Force EOD operations require EOD forces to respond outside traditional base boundaries. Air Force EOD plays a critical role in force protection by eliminating or mitigating explosive hazards created by known or suspected criminal and terrorist devices.

(3) Airfield Recovery Operations. CE rapid runway repair includes EOD operations during airfield recovery operations. The SRC plans, prioritizes, and controls all airfield recovery operations. The SRC integrates all assets (to include engineer, EOD, security forces, disaster preparedness, communications, transportation, and resource management) to support post attack recovery operations.

(4) Aerial Port Operations. Aerial ports are vital links to deploy, employ, sustain, and redeploy required forces (Service, joint, multinational) during peacetime and contingency operations. They are susceptible targets for hostile forces wishing to disrupt operations. They have a substantial EOD mission relative to the increased movement of munitions. Additionally, enemy ordnance captured for intelligence assessment must transit these ports. EOD teams respond to aerial port operations according to peace and wartime requirements to protect resources from UXOs, ensure explosive materials are safely and properly handled while in the transportation system, and ensure sound judgment is used to prevent loss or disruption of missions in an explosive hazard environment.

(5) Mortuary Services. Because of ordnance being left on or imbedded in casualties, processing casualty operations should involve EOD teams. While this is particularly important at the CONUS-port mortuaries (last military involvement prior to turning over casualties to the families), EOD teams should also support theater mortuary efforts.

(6) Base Populace Training. Air Force EOD personnel provide training on ordnance hazards and recognition, mine awareness, terrorist bomb search and recognition procedures, and personnel protective measures.

(7) DS Units (Full Capability Nuclear Support). The Air Force assigns EOD personnel dealing with nuclear munitions in personnel reliability program positions. The program is set up to review the individual's background prior to working with nuclear munitions. Personnel working in DS units with full capability nuclear support train to perform all necessary EOD actions on nuclear weapon systems from site stabilization to site recovery.

(8) Airborne Rapid Engineers Deployable Heavy Operations Repair Squadron, Engineers (REDHORSE) (ARH) capability. The Air Force airborne REDHORSE team's primary purpose is to provide limited UXO clearance capability to ARH elements to repair damaged airfields for C-130 and/or C-17 operations. An Air Force EOD element will be inserted with other members of the initial ARH assessment team during daylight hours by air insertion, air drop, and/or air-land methods. They will assess the airfield for potential landmine hazards and UXOs and clear areas of explosive hazards to allow follow-on Air Force EOD elements to be inserted and ARH team elements to be air dropped into the immediate area of the airfield. The ARH EOD team will provide limited explosive hazard clearance capability to support ARH runway repair

operations, limited force protection capability, and technical advice to the ARH flight chief on explosive hazards remaining. Consists of a 6-man team and a 2-man follow team equipped with limited EOD tools and demolition materials. They can be employed with a REDHORSE team or as a stand-alone capability.

Note: Air Force EOD forces support tactical land forces off air bases/installations in response to force protection and intelligence operations.

---

6. Training

a. Silver Flag. Training prepares EOD forces for contingency EOD operations. This 7-day course consists of classroom, practical hands-on, and field training exercises. These are integrated Civil Engineering training sites located at Tyndall (CONUS), Ramstein (Europe), and Kadena (Pacific) Air Force bases (AFBs).

b. Air Mobility Warfare Center. This center conducts "Eagle Flag" deployment exercises and EOD Combat Skills Training (CST) to meet Air Force EOD pre-deployment training requirements. The training site is located at Fort Dix, New Jersey.

c. Training references:

- Joint Nuclear EOD School
- Radiological Emergency Team Operation School
- Advanced IED Disposal (AIEDD) School
- ATF/FBI Post Blast Course
- LVBIED Course–FBI

Appendix A

MULTI-SERVICE EOD CAPABILITIES MATRIX

Table A-1. Multi-Service EOD Capabilities Matrix

Capability	Army			Navy						Air Force		Marine Corps			
	EOD Team	EOD Company	CONUS Support Company	Mobile (CSG/ESG/CES)	MCM	SOF (NSW/CIF)	VSW/MCM	Shore	OCD (NRF)	Home Base	Deployed	MEU	ESB EOD Platoon	MWSS EOD Section	Base/Station
CONVENTIONAL MUNITIONS															
Locate/Identify	X	X		X	X	X	X	X	X	X	X	X	X	X	X
RSP	X	X		X	X	X	X	X		X	X	X	X	X	X
Dispose	X	X		X	X	X	X	X	X	X	X	X	X	X	X
Near-Surface Buried Munitions Detection	X	X		X	X	X		X	X	X	X	X	X	X	X
Subsurface Buried Munitions Detection	X	X		X	X	X		X	X	X	X	X	X	X	X
Buried Ordnance Recovery	X	X		X	X	X		X	X	X	X	X	X	X	X
Large Area Munitions Clearance	X	X		X	X			X	X	X	X	X	X	X	X
Airfield Recovery	X	X		X	X	X		X		X	X	X	X	X	X
Sub-munitions Clearance	X	X		X	X	X		X	X	X	X	X	X	X	X
Surface Munitions Disruption	X	X		X	X	X		X		X	X	X	X	X	X
Munitions Storage Area Accident Cleanup	X	X		X	X			X		X	X	X	X	X	X

Table A-1. Multi-Service EOD Capabilities Matrix (continued)

Capability	Army			Navy						Air Force		Marine Corps			
	EOD Team	EOD Company	CONUS Support Company	Mobile (CSG/ESG/CES)	MCM	SOF (NSW/CIF)	VSW/MCM	Shore	OCD (NRF)	Home Base	Deployed	MEU	ESB EOD Platoon	MWSS EOD Section	Base/Station
Naval Sea Mines (1)															
Locate/Identify				X	X		X	X	X						
RSP				X	X		X	X							
Dispose				X	X		X	X	X						
Recover					X										
Low-Influence Diving				X	X		X	X(3)	X(3)						
Limpet Mines (1)															
Locate/Identify				X	X	X		X	X						
RSP				X	X			X	X						
Dispose				X	X			X	X						
Underwater Ordnance (1)															
Locate/Identify				X	X	X	X	X	X						
RSP				X	X		X	X							
Dispose				X	X		X	X	X						
Improvised Explosive Device (IED)/Vehicle Borne Improvised Explosive Device (VBIED)															
IED	X	X	X	X	X	X		X		X	X	X	X	X	X
Large VBIED	X	X	X	X	X			X		X	X	X	X	X	X
WMD															
Locate/Identify	X	X	X	X		X		X(3)		X(3)	X(3)	X(3)	X(3)	X(3)	X(3)
RSP	X	X	X(3)	X		X		X							
Nuclear Munitions															
Radiation Detection/Monitor	X	X	X	X		X		X(3)		X	X	X	X	X	X
RSP Nuclear System		X	X	X				X(3)		X		X	X	X	X
Continue RSP			X	X(3)				X(3)		X		X	X	X	X
Seal/Package			X	X				X(3)		X	X	X	X	X	X

Table A-1. Multi-Service EOD Capabilities Matrix (continued)

| Capability | Army | | | Navy | | | | | | Air Force | | Marine Corps | | | |
	EOD Team	EOD Company	CONUS Support Company	Mobile (CSG/ESG/CES)	MCM	SOF (NSW/CIF)	VSW/MCM	Shore	OCD (NRF)	Home Base	Deployed	MEU	ESB EOD Platoon	MWSS EOD Section	Base/Station
Biological Munitions															
Detection	X(3)	X(3)	X(3)			(5)									
Decontaminate	X	X	X	X		(5)		X(3)							
Seal/Package	X	X	X	X	X	(5)	X	X(3)		X	X				
RSP	X	X	X		X	(5)		X(3)		X	X	X	X	X	X
Emergency Disposal	X	X	X	X	X	(5)	X	X(3)		X	X	X	X	X	X
Chemical Munitions															
Agent Identification	X	X	X	X	X	(5)		X(3)		X	X	X	X	X	X
Agent Decontamination	X	X	X	X	X	(5)		X(3)		X	X	X	X	X	X
Seal/Package	X	X	X	X		(5)		X(3)		X	X	X	X	X	X
RSP	X	X	X	X		(5)		X(3)		X	X	X	X	X	X
Emergency Disposal	X	X	X	X	X	(5)		X(3)		X	X	X	X	X	X
Munitions Intel Gathering	X	X	X	X	X	(5)	X	X	X	X	X	X	X	X	X
Exploitation	X	X	X	X	X	(5)	X	X		X	X	X	X	X	X
Inerting						(5)						X	X	X	X
Explosive Demolition	X	X	X	X	X	(5)	X	X	X	X	X	X	X	X	X
Vessel Boarding Search & Seizure				X	X	(5)						X			
NEO	X	X	X	X	X	(5)		X(3)			X	X	X	X	

Capability	Army			Navy						Air Force		Marine Corps			
	EOD Team	EOD Company	CONUS Support Company	Mobile (CSG/ESG/CES)	MCM	SOF (NSW/CIF)	VSW/MCM	Shore	OCD (NRF)	Home Base	Deployed	MEU	ESB EOD Platoon	MWSS EOD Section	Base/Station
TRAP/Combat Search and Rescue				X		X						X	X	X	
Aircraft Crash Recovery	X	X	X	X						X	X	X	X	X	X
VIP Protection	X	X	X	X	X	X		X		X	X	X	X	X	X
Dynamic Entry	X(4)	X(4)	X(4)			X						X(4)	X(4)	X(4)	X(4)
Tactical Insert/Extract Personnel and Equipment															
Parachute				X		X				X(3)	X(3)	X	X		
SPIE				X	X	X		X		X(3)	X(3)	X	X	X	X
Fast Rope	X(3)			X	X	X		X		X(3)	X(3)	X	X	X	X
Rappel	X(3)			X	X	X		X		X(3)	X(3)	X	X	X	X
Combat Rubber Raiding Craft				X	X	X	X	X				X			
Casting				X	X	X		X				X			
Robotics (Small)	X	X		X		X		X	X	X	X	X	X	X	X
Robotics (Large)	X	X	X	X				X		X	X	X	X	X	X
Satellite Communications	X	X		X	X	X	X	X	X			X	X		
Organic Tactical Communications	X	X	X	X	X	X	X	X	X	X	X	X	X	X	

Note (1): In water only, otherwise treat as conventional ordnance.

Note (2): Refer to established OPLANs for further guidance.

Note (3): Selected detachments only.

Note (4): See Service chapters for unique breaching capabilities.

Note (5): To fully understand these mission capabilities contact theater special operations commander.

Appendix B

EOD PLANNING CHECKLIST FOR JOINT OPERATIONS

1. Mobilization Planning

a. Train, equip, and organize EOD forces within each Service component.

b. Review OPLANs for EOD UTC requirements (personnel and equipment) to include the planned flow of EOD forces time-phased force deployment data (TPFDD).

c. Consider adding an EOD-qualified officer to the combatant commander's special staff and subordinate joint force special staff.

d. Identify opportunities for joint EOD operations in exercise plans, OPLANs, contingency plans, and OPORDs.

e. Perform an intelligence estimate of information necessary to counter the UXO and IED threat including:

    (1) Ordnance orders of battle.

    (2) Terrorist/paramilitary threats and capabilities.

    (3) Critical target listing (enemy) and munitions US forces plan to use.

    (4) Critical vulnerabilities (friendly) and what munitions the enemy may use.

f. Coordinate periodic joint, interoperability exercises with multi-Service EOD forces.

2. Deployment Planning

a. Update intelligence estimate.

b. Update mission analysis to determine EOD UTCs to support the mission requirements, to include:

    (1) Service EOD requirements.

    (2) Multinational EOD mission requirements.

    (3) Total EOD requirements.

c. Source joint or Service specific EOD capabilities through JOPES to support the combatant commander requirements. Sources of EOD support:

    (1) US military EOD forces.

    (2) Multinational and/or host nation EOD forces.

    (3) Contracted EOD organizations.

d. Determine flow of EOD forces (TPFDD).

3. Employment Planning

a. Develop mission statements and concept of operations.

    (1) Identify single-Service EOD missions (see chapters III-VI).

    (2) Identify joint EOD missions (see chapter II).

(3) Select employment options for conducting joint operations (see chapter II).

    (a) Service responsibility with DIRLAUTH.

    (b) Lead-Service component (with or without TACON/OPCON).

    (c) Subordinate EOD JTF.

b. Establish JEODOC (if required) (see chapter II and appendix C).

c. Ensure methodology is in place for intelligence collection and dissemination.

    (1) Disseminate new or unknown ordnance technical information within theater.

    (2) Process new or unknown ordnance items to appropriate agencies outside theater.

    (3) Coordinate with the National Geospatial-Intelligence Agency for updated mapping, geodesy, and multi-spectral imagery data covering the area of the UXO/EOD incident.

d. Establish authorized demolition areas for UXO and other explosive hazards in accordance with applicable host nation, US, and DOD explosive safety and environmental protection laws and regulations.

4. Sustainment Planning

a. Coordinate administrative and logistical support with theater support command or Service components.

b. Monitor EOD reports; take action as required.

5. Redeployment Planning

a. Ensure EOD/wing commanders understand and employ appropriate procedures (i.e., explosives safety and environmental protection) for the closing of demolition areas.

b. Establish EOD battle hand-off requirements and procedures.

    (1) To host nation.

    (2) To multinational EOD forces.

    (3) To civilian contractors.

c. Determine redeployment flow of EOD forces using JOPES.

d. Conduct post-mission analysis.

e. Reconstitution of forces.

Appendix C

ESTABLISHING AN EOD JTF

1. Background

A key responsibility of the geographic combatant commander is the designation of an EOD controlling authority after a full evaluation of the assigned mission. It is vital to the effectiveness of the TF that the EOD JTF commander, deputy commander, operations officer and other key operations and planning staff members are qualified EOD officers. All personnel assigned to the EOD JTF staff should understand multi-Service or joint TTP to allow for a seamless transition. EOD JTF planning should be in concert with established joint doctrine as found in JP 5-00.2, *Joint Task Force Planning Guidance and Procedures*.

2. Authority

Establishment of an EOD JTF is appropriate when EOD C2 requirements exceed the capabilities of the JFC or lead Service EOD staff or when conducting EOD operations with a joint force would be more efficient. The JFC normally forms an EOD JTF from the nucleus of the designated major Service component EOD command. Both the Army and Navy have existing C2 EOD units around which an EOD JTF is built. Specifically, using the Army's EOD group (0-6 command) headquarters, or the Navy's mobile group (0-6 command), provides a ready EOD headquarters unit to serve as a building block for an EOD JTF headquarters. A combatant commander or subordinate JFC establishes an EOD JTF. When formed, the EOD JTF is a temporary joint EOD headquarters that controls two or more different Service component's EOD units in a specific JOA to accomplish the EOD mission. The EOD JTF supports the theater campaign plan, JTF mission, or other operations as directed.

3. Responsibilities

The EOD JTF is responsible for making recommendations to the senior JFC (senior JTF commander, sub-unified command commander or geographic combatant commander) on the proper employment of EOD and for accomplishing assigned operational missions. The EOD JTF develops a detailed plan using the JOPES for integrated employment of assigned and attached forces based on an assessment of the operational requirements.

a. Organization of Forces. The commander, EOD JTF, has the authority to organize assigned or attached forces to meet mission requirements.

b. Commander's Guidance. The combatant commander is responsible for:

(1) Defining the scope of responsibility of the EOD JTF.

(2) Defining units attached OPCON or TACON, and relationships within the JFC.

(3) Defining EOD JTF's JOA and specific missions within the JOA to include specific responsibility.

(4) Ensuring that all identified external support requirements to include security support for sustaining the EOD force are properly coordinated.

4. The EOD JTF Staff

The designated EOD commander coordinates the establishment of the EOD JTF staff. A doctrinal method is to develop EOD JTF staffs around the "core" of the designated EOD commander's assigned staff. Other Service EOD personnel augment the designated EOD JTF's core staff. The geographic combatant commander may also provide certain augmentation (to include security, medical, and administration/logistics) to an EOD JTF, depending on the mission and support requirements. See Figure C-1, Notional EOD JTF Staff Organization.

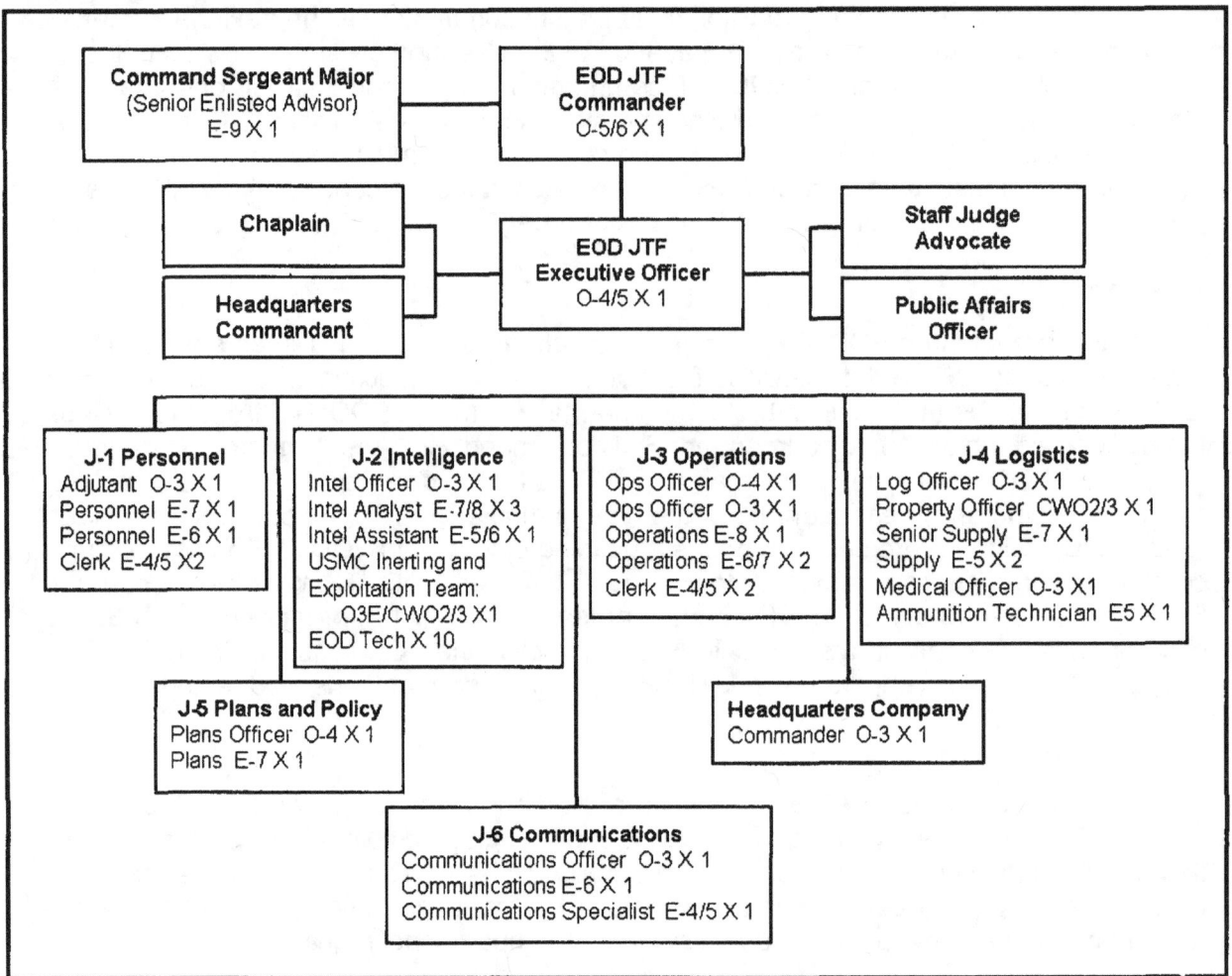

Figure C-1. Notional EOD JTF Staff Organization

a. Organization. EOD commanders organize the EOD JTF staff as necessary to carry out assigned duties and responsibilities. The EOD JTF staff includes at a minimum the normal J-1 through J-4 staff and may include J-5 and J-6 as well as special staff members as required.

b. Orientation Program. A staff orientation program ensures that all individuals assigned to the EOD JTF become thoroughly familiar with multi-Service and joint EOD operations. This can be accomplished through the establishment of a joint reception center, a short training program, or even use of a "buddy" system whereby an experienced EOD JTF staff member mentors a newly assigned individual.

5. Staff Functions and Responsibilities

a. The Manpower and Personnel Directorate (J-1). The J-1 provides joint personnel planning, coordination, management, and review; assists subordinate commands in acquiring, replacing, and transferring personnel; provides administrative and personnel service; monitors and reports the personnel readiness of assigned, allocated, and apportioned forces to higher headquarters; and provides appropriate input to OPLANs.

b. The Intelligence Directorate (J-2). The primary function of the J-2 is to support the EOD JTF staff and subordinate assigned/attached units by ensuring the availability of reliable intelligence and timely indications and warning on the characteristics of UXO/IED on the battlefield, first-seen ordnance, and potential terrorist threats. Members of the directorate actively participate in joint staff planning and in planning, coordinating, directing, integrating, and controlling a concentration of intelligence efforts on the proper enemy items-of-intelligence interest at the appropriate time. The J-2 also has the functional responsibility for the acquisition, production, requests, and dissemination of intelligence and counterintelligence to support EOD operations. The J-2 develops, refines, and updates the EOD JTF intelligence estimate to provide a common understanding and view of the battlefield and directs intelligence collection efforts and exploitation of first-seen/recovered foreign ordnance. The EOD JTF J-2 also analyzes enemy IED TTP and provides to the EOD J-3, subordinate EOD units, and senior JFC, specific weapons/IED information and UXO/IED trends, as well as possible countermeasures. The J-2 serves as the single POC within intelligence channels for the collection and dissemination of technical intelligence products and provides intelligence input to OPORDs.

c. The Operations Directorate (J-3). The J-3 conducts short-range planning functions, coordinates and integrates EOD operations within the entire JOA. Should the EOD JTF not include a J-5, the J-3 would also perform long-range functions. The J-3 conducts crisis action planning; assists the J-5 (if organized) in deliberate planning; and coordinates and directs the deployment, employment, and redeployment of assigned and attached forces. The J-3 is responsible for providing oversight of current operations and planning for emerging missions; maintaining a current operations estimate; preparing operational plans, annexes, orders, reports, and records; determining pre-deployment technical training requirements for replacement EOD personnel; and recommending EOD priorities for operational support, task organization, and JTF boundaries. J-3 will also monitor and keep contact with Service EOD units and when necessary, may coordinate through the applicable Service component to have these Service-controlled EOD units to perform specific EOD actions outside their normal Service EOD mission. Should the EOD JTF not include a J-6, the J-3 would also perform the C4I planning and execution functions.

d. The Logistics Directorate (J-4). The J-4 provides logistic oversight for internal EOD JTF logistics functions and monitors and manages readiness issues. The J-4 formulates logistics plans and coordinates supply, maintenance, transportation, field services, general engineering, health services, contracting, host-nation support, and other logistics activities from the designated unit(s) providing logistic support to the EOD JTF.

e. The Plans Directorate (J-5). The J-5, if not combined with the J-3, conducts deliberate planning for the EOD JTF, develops and recommends C2 arrangements, and participates in the JTF, theater, or combatant commander's campaign and concept planning. The J-5 also projects future EOD requirements for personnel, material, and organization. When required, the J-5 provides the EOD JTF input for the JOPES.

f. The C4I Systems Directorate (J-6). The J-6 is responsible to coordinate communications, electronics, and automated information systems support within and to the

EOD JTF. This includes development and integration of C4I architecture and plans that support the command's operational and strategic requirements as well as policy and guidance for implementation and integration of interoperable C4I systems to exercise command in the execution of the EOD JTF mission.

g. Staff Judge Advocate (SJA). An EOD JTF may or may not have a dedicated SJA staff, but in all cases must have an SJA advisor identified to provide legal advice. The SJA is the legal advisor on issues ranging from administrative law to rules of engagement. To ensure the EOD JTF complies with international law, domestic law, environmental protection laws, and DOD regulations, the SJA coordinates with the JTF SJA and EOD JTF supported commands. The SJA also advises the commander and staff on compliance with environmental laws, regulations, treaties, conventions, status-of-forces agreements (SOFAs) and their potential impact on operations. Specifically, the combatant command SJA and JTF SJA are responsible for legal support in the development of the "Environmental Considerations" annex to an OPLAN and/or OPORD to ensure that legal requirements related to environmental considerations are incorporated as appropriate.

h. Public Affairs Officer (PAO). An EOD JTF may or may not have a dedicated PAO staff. If the EOD JTF has its own PAO, it would perform PAO functions as described in JP 5-00.2.

i. Chaplain. It is unlikely that an EOD JTF would have chaplain on its staff. Normally, EOD JTF personnel will receive religious support from the Service chaplain(s) responsible for religious support within the JOA. There is a high probability that during war EOD personnel will require the services of a chaplain due to the fact EOD personnel perform mortuary operations and have direct contact with fatalities (e.g., aircraft crashes, IED post blast analysis, and major accident responses).

j. HQ Commandant/Internal Support Coordinator. The EOD JTF commander appoints the HQ commandant/internal support coordinator who is responsible for all aspects of the headquarters operation. The commandant/internal support coordinator assumes the initial functional responsibility for all equipment and facilities assigned to the EOD JTF and assigns subsequent functions to personnel and agencies in direct control of those activities.

Appendix D
STANDARDIZED EOD REPORTS

1. Background

Timely and accurate UXO/IED reporting and intelligence information gathering during EOD operations, regardless of Service component, is critical to the safe conduct of operations within an area of responsibility. Although reporting procedures are similar between the Service components and provide similar information, submission and dissemination procedures differ. Timely, standardized reporting and dissemination provide multi-Service EOD forces with the ability to effectively counter the hazards associated with ordnance. During multi-Service operations, using the following reports prevents redundancy and ensures accurate EOD incident tasking, reporting, and tracking.

2. Explosive Hazard (EH) Spot Report

a. Purpose. The EH Spot Report is a detailed, two-way reporting system that makes clear where the UXO/IED hazard areas are, the priority for clearance, and which units the hazard affects. The report is used to request help in handling a UXO/IED hazard that affects the unit's mission and is beyond their ability to handle. This report helps the commander set priorities based on the battlefield situation. The EH Spot Report is the first echelon report sent when an observer detects UXO/IED. The report consists of nine lines and is sent by the fastest means available (Table D-1).

b. Routing. Forward the EH Spot Report through the chain of command. Each commander in the chain who reviews the report may change the priority to reflect the current tactical situation or projected battle plans. Each commander in the chain is responsible for forwarding EH Spot Reports through command channels and for setting the proper priority for each report. A higher-level commander in the chain that changes a priority must inform subordinate commands, especially the initial reporting unit. In addition to the priority status, all commanders need to be kept informed of the status of each UXO/IED hazard in their area. The reporting unit's higher headquarters that is supported by EOD determines the final priority. Based on METT-T, with the Army adding a "C" for civil considerations, EOD teams use the EH spot reports to prioritize and sequence their response to assigned UXO/IED incidents.

Table D-1. Sample Explosive Hazard Spot Report

Line 1.	Date-Time Group (DTG): DTG item was discovered.
Line 2.	Reporting Activity: Unit identification code and location (8-digit grid of UXO/IED).
Line 3.	Contact Method: Radio frequency, call sign, POC, and telephone number.
Line 4.	Type of Ordnance: Dropped, projected, placed, possible IED, or thrown. If available, give the size of the hazard area and number of items, if more than one. Without touching, disturbing, or approaching (due to a potential tripwire) the item, include details about size, shape, color, and condition (intact or leaking).
Line 5.	CBRNE Contamination: Be as specific as possible.
Line 6.	Resources Threatened: Report any equipment, facilities, or other assets that are threatened.
Line 7.	Impact on Mission: Provide a short description of your current tactical situation and how the presence of the UXO/IED affects your status.
Line 8.	Protective Measures: Describe any measures taken to protect personnel and equipment.
Line 9.	Recommended Priority: Recommend a priority for response by EOD technicians.
Priority	**Basis**
Immediate	Stops the unit's maneuver and mission capability, or threatens critical assets vital to the mission.
Indirect	Slows the unit's maneuver and mission capability, or threatens critical assets important to the mission.
Minor	Reduces the unit's maneuver and mission capability, or threatens noncritical assets of value.
No Threat	Has little or no affect on the unit's capabilities or assets.

3. EOD Incident Report

The EOD unit responding to the incident submits its approved electronic report in digital format. Table D-2 provides the minimum amount of information that should be included in the report but is not the format of the electronic EOD incident report. The EOD unit should immediately report essential details of the operation that have immediate and vital significance. Include the following relevant information in the EOD incident report.

Table D-2. Sample EOD Incident Report

Line 1.	Responding EOD unit.
Line 2.	Personnel, vehicles, and any special equipment responding to incident.
Line 3.	Site POC or on-scene commander.
Line 4.	Geographical location (latitude/longitude and/or Global Positioning System) and location with respect to buildings or valuable installations.
Line 5.	Chronological record of operations, including safety precautions taken.
Line 6.	Detailed description and available photographs/drawings of items; positive identification; external markings/condition of case or body; worn or damaged parts; corrosion; extent and kind of sea growth; condition of explosives; fuzing/firing mechanisms; batteries; important components or fittings; and antistripping devices or booby traps.
Line 7.	Reason object failed to function as designed.
Line 8.	Difficulties or unusual circumstances related to the incident.
Line 9.	RSP used, if applicable.
Line 10.	Final disposition of items.
Line 11.	List expenditure of demolition materials.
Line 12.	Additional pertinent information.

Note: This report does not supersede, unless specified, specific Service reporting requirements.

4. Technical Intelligence Reports.

Technical intelligence reporting follows the appropriate Service procedures contained in Army Technical Manual/Air Force Technical Order/Navy EOD Bulletin 60A-1-1-7.

5. Lead Service and EOD JTF EOD Report.

Each Service maintains unique, Service-specific EOD reports and formats. It is useful when conducting operations as a joint force to have a single reporting format/system. Those EOD assets under TACON/OPCON of lead Service or EOD JTF prepare the following intelligence reports for first-seen ordnance:

a.   Spot Report. The acquiring unit prepares the spot report as an oral or written report. The sender transmits the report by the fastest means available. The minimum information requirements for this report are as follows:

(1) Identification of reporting unit.

(2) What is being reported (for instance ordnance or documents).

b.   Preliminary Technical Report (PRETECHREP) Type B (table D-3). An EOD unit forwards this report when an item of ordnance has technical intelligence value. The sender of the report forwards the report to the JEODOC/EOD JTF J-2. An interim RSP is developed and reported, whether the RSP is issued or not.

Table D-3. Unclassified Sample PRETECHREP

For the protection of sources and methods and unless otherwise directed by on-scene intelligence personnel, the initial report shall be classified SECRET/NOFORN/WNINTEL. WARNING NOTICE – INTELLIGENCE SOURCES OR METHODS INVOLVED. The first paragraph of the report shall read:

1. (U) This report is initially classified S/NOFORN/WNINTEL for protection of sources and methods. Verification of correct classification by (your Service intelligence organization) is required.

Foreign nuclear weapons or components, including sabotage devices, are evacuated through technical intelligence channels. Security classification of such items, once in evacuation channels, will not be lower than SECRET (RESTRICTED DATA).

PRIORITY

FM: XXXX ORD CO (EOD)
TO: XXXX (JEODOC)
INFO: CDRUSATECHDET INDIAN HEAD MD
NAVEODTECHDIV INDIAN HEAD MD//
FSTC CHARLOTTESVILLE VA//AIFRCB/AIFIM//
DIA WASHINGTON DC//DT2C/DT-3B//

BT
SECRET/NOFORN/WNINTEL
WARNING NOTICE - SENSITIVE INTELLIGENCE SOURCES OR METHODS INVOLVED

SUBJ: PRETECHREP

REF A. MSG XXX SUBJECT: SPOT REPORT

a. ( ) DATE FOUND, LOCATION (map references)
b. ( ) TYPE OF EQUIPMENT AND QUANTITY
c. ( ) ORIGIN
d. ( ) BRIEF DESCRIPTION WITH DISTINGUISHING MARKS
e. ( ) TECHNICAL CHARACTERISTICS WITH AN IMMEDIATE VALUE
f. ( ) NAME OF COMMANDER OF CAPTURING UNIT
g. ( ) TIME AND ORIGIN OF MESSAGE
h. ( ) TENTATIVE RSP (EOD use only)

(Classification)

NOTE: The subject and each paragraph and subparagraph must be classified individually, but not higher than the classification of the entire message.

Examples: 1. (S/NF); 2. (U)

c. Complementary Technical Report (COMTECHREP) Type B.

(1) Purpose. Use the COMTECHREP Type B to report information about explosive ordnance. TECHINT teams prepare these reports, as do EOD personnel. However, EOD personnel only prepare them in the absence of a TECHINT team or when requested by a G-2 or representative. This report must be as complete and detailed as possible. EOD personnel prepare and send this report by the fastest means through the JEODOC/EOD JTF J-2 to the TECHINT unit.

(2) Timing and Completeness. Complete all of the items in the report that you have information for and strive for the most complete report possible. However, when a detailed report might result in serious delay and the report is of significant or new items of extreme urgency, complete only paragraphs a-e, l(1), y, and aa of priority message. See table D-4

(3) Additional Information. Additional paragraphs of particular importance, for example, those referring to safety (paragraph u) or design (paragraph m) may be included at the originator's discretion. Paragraph aa should state an estimated time required for a detailed report to be completed.

Table D-4. Unclassified Sample COMTECHREP

PRIORITY

FM: XXXX ORD CO (EOD)
TO: XXXX (JEODOC)
INFO: CDRUSATECHDET INDIAN HEAD MD
NAVEODTECHDIV INDIAN HEAD MD//
FSTC CHARLOTTESVILLE VA//AIFRCB/AIFIM//
DIA WASHINGTON DC//DT2C/DT-3B//

BT
SECRET/NOFORN/WNINTEL
WARNING NOTICE - SENSITIVE INTELLIGENCE SOURCES OR METHODS INVOLVED

SUBJ: COMTECHREP

REF A. MSG XXX SUBJECT: PRETECHREP

a. ( ) Date and location of acquisition, acquired by, and for whom.
b. ( ) Nationality, designation, and identification marks.
c. ( ) Description.
d. ( ) Overall length, including fuze, tail, vanes, or control surfaces and fittings; measurement of various states (if there are several).
e. ( ) Maximum diameter of each state (if there are several).
f. ( ) Shape, design, and internal configuration (streamlining shells).
g. ( ) Span of vanes and control surfaces.
h. ( ) Number, relative positions, and dimensions (width, length, size, and/or configuration of control surfaces).
i. ( ) Thickness of casing at —
   (1) ( ) nose.
   (2) ( ) slides.
   (3) ( ) base.
j. ( ) Type and materials of body and control surfaces.
k. ( ) Color and markings of —
   (1) ( ) nose.
   (2) ( ) body.

(3)　( ) tail and vanes.

l.　( ) Weight —

  (1)　total, including propellant.

  (2)　( ) of filling.

m. ( ) Nature of filling. If chemical or biological warfare in nature, give method of filling, for example, bomblets or massive fill; specify method of delivery, such as spray, roundburst, or airburst. For antitank missiles with high explosive antitank (HEAT) warheads, give full details of cone-liner materials, cone angle, and diameter. For antitank missiles with non-HEAT warheads, give full description of the warhead.

n. ( ) Type of missile guidance system and method of stabilization environment (control and guidance radars, acquisition radar); frequencies used for reception response (in case of a transponder); and proximity fuze (if there is one). Electronic countermeasures and electronic counter-countermeasures equipment and/or chaff-dispensing equipment.

o. ( ) Sensors.

p. ( ) Diameter of radome and size of homing dish, if fitted.

q. ( ) Dimensions (internal and external) of wave guides in the homing head and wave guides and/or aerials in the wings or body, and the technology used.

r. ( ) Homing head, transducer design, and shape and size (torpedoes).

s. ( ) Method of propulsion and propeller data (torpedoes).

t. ( ) Detonating system, fuzing system (nose, tail, or transverse) and firing mechanism details.

u. ( ) Type of suspension, giving details of devices used, such as electrically operated hoods or release gear.

v. ( ) Antihandling or booby-trap devices.

w. ( ) Other information (to include estimate of time required to prepare item for shipment to TECHINT center or designated industrial firm for detailed analysis).

x. ( ) Name of officer in command of technical team making examination.

y. ( ) Time and origin of message.

z. ( ) Energy used for mobile systems other than propulsions.

aa.　( ) Estimate of time required for completion.

Note: If feasible, a preliminary set of photographs should be sent with the report.

(Classification)

Note: The subject and each paragraph and subparagraph must be classified individually, but not higher than the classification of the entire message.

---

6. Responsibilities

a.　Service Responsibility (with DIRLAUTH). DIRLAUTH as authorized by CJTF allows for more rapid dissemination of ordnance intelligence between Service EOD forces prior to submitting reports into intelligence channels. Each Service EOD command must coordinate with other EOD assets to disseminate this information.

b.　JEODOC. The JEODOC, when established, is responsible for the collection of incident tracking reports and ordnance intelligence from Service component EOD assets, assessment and dissemination of information to all Service EOD assets within the AO, and submission of consolidated information reports to intelligence channels.

c. EOD JTF. The EOD JTF collects incident tracking reports and ordnance intelligence from Service-component EOD assets, assesses and disseminates information to all Service EOD assets within the AO, and submits consolidated information reports to intelligence channels.

Appendix E

EOD RECURRING SUPPORT OPERATIONS

1. Background

The DOD EOD force performs numerous support missions on a recurring basis. Each of the Services' EOD personnel assists in the performance of these missions. Service-specific missions, capabilities, and non-recurring support are identified in the appropriate Service section of this publication.

2. Recurring DOD EOD Support Missions

The DOD EOD force performs the following missions on a recurring basis:

a. VIPPSA.

(1) Currently the DOS and DOD use joint EOD assets to support the USSS and the DOS in protecting the President or Vice President of the United States (POTUS/VPOTUS) and their immediate families (as defined by DOD Instruction 5030.34). This protection is also provided to the US Secretary of State, foreign heads of state, prime ministers, ministers of defense, other VIPs, and/or NSSEs, for example, the United Nations General Assembly, as specified by the President of the United States. The EOD force provides specific protection from all potentially hazardous explosive devices within assigned secure areas for protecting VIPs.

(2) The Secretary of the Army is the DOD EA for the direct receipt, approval, coordination, and tasking of USSS and DOS requests for routine reimbursable and no reimbursable (primarily being the POTUS and VPOTUS) EOD protective support for locations worldwide. The Assistant Secretary of the Army (Installations, Logistics, and Environment) maintains oversight of this support on behalf of the EA. The Joint Director of Military Support provides staff support to the Secretary of the Army to assist in carrying out this executive agency. Commander, US Joint Forces Command (USJFCOM), is designated the operating agent to act on behalf of the EA to plan, coordinate, task, and execute routine EOD VIP protective support employing assets from the military Services and the unified and specified commands. The US Army EOD for VIPPSA, Fort Gillem, Georgia, is the tasking and coordinating agent for the Commander, USJFCOM.

(3) Support requests from USSS or DOS are communicated directly to the VIPPSA. For missions within CONUS, the VIPPSA identifies the closest EOD unit (of any Service) and tasks that unit's command to provide EOD teams to support the USSS or DOS security details. For OCONUS missions, the VIPPSA tasks the geographical combatant commander to provide EOD teams. EOD teams assigned to support USSS or DOS are subject to overall supervision and direction of the USSS Director or the Director of the DOS Office of Diplomatic Security (or their authorized representative) at the mission site for the duration of the support mission.

(4) A typical EOD VIP support mission will include the following tasks:

(a) Conduct a site survey of areas to be visited by the protectee.

(b) Assist in establishing evacuation routes for potentially hazardous explosive devices.

(c) Search the areas to be visited by the protectee for hazardous explosive devices.

(d) Clear the protectees' departure route in the event a hazardous explosive device is discovered.

(5) If the EOD team discovers a hazardous explosive device, it provides technical assistance to local law enforcement agencies/bomb disposal teams as requested.

b. Since criminal and terrorist attacks commonly involve the use of explosive devices on US forces, force commanders should include EOD commanders/planners in all force protection planning and training. During periods of conflict, the awareness of, and emphasis on, force protection are heightened, thus increasing EOD response to potentially hazardous situations. In addition to actual response to explosive devices, EOD forces can provide training in UXO/IED recognition and reporting; bomb threat search procedures and evacuation; site vulnerability assessments, and SOP preparation and validation. This training will increase the effectiveness of the commander's force protection program. EOD forces also provide DS to NEO forces.

c. Joint POW/MIA Accounting Command (JPAC) is a standing task force under the Commander Pacific Command (PACOM). EOD personnel support the JPAC by providing the fullest possible accounting of US personnel listed as missing in action. Most sites investigated by JPAC teams are littered with UXO from military action, or in the case of aircraft crash sites, from UXO that was part of the aircraft's payload. EOD personnel clear UXO from investigation sites so that JPAC recovery personnel can operate in a safe environment. EOD support to this mission is provided by all Services.

d. Certain EOD units have special capabilities and training to recognize and render safe all known types of WMD. All EOD units are trained to provide first response to suspected WMD and to assist in coordination of responses by more specialized national WMD response assets.

e. EOD forces perform technical intelligence gathering and reporting on new or first-seen foreign ordnance, aircraft, weapons systems, or sabotage devices encountered by maneuver forces.

f. EOD forces develop training programs and conduct humanitarian demining operations (HDO) training in support of SOF in developing countries that are experiencing landmine/UXO problems.

g. EOD forces conduct inspections of weapon/ammunition storage sites during peacekeeping operations for compliance with peace agreements. EOD forces assist with the safety and storage requirements for ammunition and associated components.

h. EOD forces inspect and destroy foreign ammunition and explosive items.

i. Amnesty Programs. EOD units assist in the collection and disposal of hazardous munitions and components as part of the maneuver commander's force protection program to ensure the continued safety of military personnel.

j. Accident/Incident/Post Blast Investigation. EOD forces provide technical information on foreign and US ordnance and conduct crater or munition fragmentation analysis, as part of an accident or incident investigation.

REFERENCES

Joint Publications

JP 0-2, *Unified Action Armed Forces (UNAAF),* 10 July 2001

JP 1-02, *Department of Defense Dictionary of Military and Associated Terms,* 12 April 2001 (As Amended Through 9 May 2005)

JP 3-0, *Doctrine for Joint Operations,* 10 September 2001

JP 3-07, *Joint Doctrine for Military Operations Other than War,* 16 June 1995

JP 3-07.2, *Joint Tactics, Techniques, and Procedures for Antiterrorism,* 17 March 1998

JP 3-07.5, *Joint Tactics, Techniques, and Procedures for Non-Combatant Evacuation Operations,* 30 September 1997

JP 3-15, *Joint Doctrine for Barriers, Obstacles, and Mine Warfare,* 24 February 1999

JP 5-0, *Doctrine for Planning Joint Operations,* 13 April 1995

JP 5-00.2, *Joint Task Force Planning Guidance and Procedures,* 13 January 1999

DOD Instruction 5030.34, *Agreement Between the United States Secret Service and the Department of Defense Concerning Protection of the President and other Officials,* 17 September 1986

DOD Directive 3150.8, *DOD Response to Radiological Accidents,* 13 June 1996

DOD Directive 3150.8-M, *Nuclear Weapon Accident Response Procedures (NARP),* 22 February 2005

Technical Manual (TM) (Army), Technical Order (TO) (Air Force), EOD Bulletin (Navy), 60A-1-1-7, *Explosive Ordnance Disposal Procedures; Field Evaluation and Intelligence,* 23 March 1999

Multi-Service

AR 75-14/MCO 8027.1D/OPNAVINST 8027.1G/AFJI 32-3002, *Interservice Responsibilities and Procedures for Explosive Ordnance Disposal,* 14 February 1992

FM 3-100.38, MCRP 3-17.2B, NTTP 3-02.41, AFTTP(I) 3-2.12, *MultiService Procedures for Unexploded Ordnance,* date

FM 6-02.85 (FM 101-4), MCRP 3-40.2A, NTTP 3-13.1.16, AFTTP(I) 3-2.22, *MultiService Procedures for Joint Task Force—Information Management,* 10 Sep 03

Army

> **NOTE:** The new Army numbering system for field manuals reflects the new number, followed by the old number in parenthesis.

AR 75-15, *Explosive Ordnance Disposal,* 22 February 2005

FM 4-30.5, *Explosive Ordnance Disposal Operations,* 28 April 2005

FM 3-24.32 (FM 20-32), *Mine/Countermine Operations,* 2 February 2004

FM 4-30.11 (FM 21-16), *Unexploded Ordnance Procedures,* 30 August 1994

FM 3-34.2, *Combined Arms Breaching Operations,* 31 August 2000

Marine Corps

MCWP 3-2, *Aviation Operations,* April 1999

MCWP 3-16, *Techniques and Procedures for Fire Support Planning/Coordination,* March 1992

MCWP 3-17.2, *Explosive Ordnance Disposal,* December 1993

MCRP 3-17.2A, *UXO Procedures,* August 1994

MCWP 3-33.6, *Humanitarian Operations,* October 1994

MCWP 3-35.3, *Military Operations on Urbanized Terrain,* April 1998

MCO 3571.2, *Explosive Ordnance Disposal Program,* August 1990

Navy

Department of the Navy, *US Navy Explosive Ordnance Disposal Plan,* 28 March 1997

OPNAVINST 3501.97, *Projected Operational Environment and Required Operational Capabilities for Explosive Ordnance Disposal Ground Forces,* 26 January 1996

NWP 3-02.4, *Explosive Ordnance Disposal,* July 1997

Air Force

AFDD 2-4, *Combat Support,* 23 March 2005

AFI 10-210, *Prime Base Engineer Emergency Force (BEEF) Program,* 1 October 2004

AFPD 32-30, *Explosive Ordnance Disposal,* 20 July 1994

AFMAN 32-3001, *EOD Program,* 1 June 1998

ANGI 32-3001, *Air National Guard Explosive Ordnance Disposal (EOD) Very Important Persons Protection Support Activity (VIPPSA) Program,* 13 May 2003

AFEOD Equipment and Supplies Listing, July 2005

GLOSSARY

PART I – ABBREVIATIONS AND ACRONYMS

A

AA&D	Advanced Access and Disablement
ADCON	administrative control
AEDT	Advanced Explosives Destruction Technique
AEIT	Advanced Explosive Investigative Technique
AFB	Air Force Base
AFDC	Air Force Doctrine Center
AFFOR	Air Force Forces
AFI	Air Force Instruction
AIEDD	Advanced IED Disposal
ALSA	Air Land Sea Application
AMCM	airborne mine countermeasures
AO	area of operations
AR	Army Regulation
ARC	Air Reserve Components
ARFOR	Army Forces
ARG	amphibious ready group
ARH	Airborne Rapid Engineers Deployable Heavy Operations Repair Squadron, Engineers
ASD	area search detachment
ATF	Bureau of Alcohol, Tobacco and Firearms (TREAS)

B

BCE	base civil engineer
BCT	brigade combat team
BN	battalion

C

C2	command and control
C3	command, control, and communications
C4I	command, control, communications, computers, and intelligence
CATF	commander, amphibious task force
CBRNE	chemical, biological, radiological, nuclear and high-yield explosives
CE	civil engineering
CEA	captured enemy ammunition

CES	combat expeditionary support
CIF	Commanders In-Extremis Force
CJTF	commander, joint task force
CO	company
COCOM	combatant command (command authority)
COMTECHREP	complementary technical report
CONUS	continental United States
CQB	Close Quarters Battle
CRRC	combat rubber raiding craft
CSB (ME)	combat support brigade (ME)
CSG	carrier strike group
CST	Combat Skills Training

D

DA	direct action
DIRLAUTH	direct liaison authorized
DOD	Department of Defense
DOS	Department of State
DS	direct support
DTG	date-time group

E

EA	executive agent
EH	explosive hazard
EOD	explosive ordnance disposal
EODMU	explosive ordnance disposal mobile unit
EODTEU	explosive ordnance disposal training and evaluation unit
ESB	engineer support battalion
ESG	expeditionary strike group

F

FAST	Fleet Antiterrorist Security Team
FBI	Federal Bureau of Investigation

G

G-2	Army or Marine Corps component intelligence staff officer (Army division or higher staff, Marine Corps brigade or higher staff)
G-3	Army or Marine Corps component operations staff officer (Army division or higher staff; Marine Corps brigade or higher staff)
GATOR	Global Antiterrorism Operational Readiness Course
GP	group

GS   general support

H

HAZWOPER   Hazardous Waste Operator
HDO   humanitarian demining operations
HEAT   high explosive antitank
HMMWV   high mobility multipurpose wheeled vehicle
HQ   headquarters

I

IDN   Initial Distribution Number
IED   improvised explosive device
IM   information management

J

J-1   manpower and personnel directorate of a joint staff
J-2   intelligence directorate of a joint staff
J-3   operations directorate of a joint staff
J-4   logistics directorate of a joint staff
J-5   plans directorate of a joint staff
J-6   command, control, communications, and computer systems directorate of a joint staff
JEODOC   joint explosive ordnance disposal operations center
JFC   joint force commander
JOA   joint operations area
JOPES   Joint Operation Planning and Execution System
JSOTF   Joint Special Operations Task Force
JTF   joint task force

L

LNO   liaison officer

M

MACA   military assistance to civil authorities
MAGTF   Marine air-ground task force
MAJCOM   major command
MARFOR   Marine Forces
MARFORLANT   Marine Forces, Atlantic
MARFORPAC   Marine Forces, Pacific
MAW   Marine aircraft wing
MCCDC   US Marine Corps Combat Development Command

MCD	mobile communications detachment
MCIEast	Marine Corps Installations East
MCIWest	Marine Corps Installations West
MCM	mine countermeasures
MCO	Marine Corps order
MCPDS	Marine Corps Publication Distribution System
MDMP	military decision making process
MDSU	mobile diving and salvage unit
ME	maneuver enhancement
MEF	Marine expeditionary force
METT-T	mission, enemy, terrain and weather, troops and support available--time available
METT-TC	mission, enemy, terrain and weather, time, troops available and civil considerations (Army only)
MEU	Marine expeditionary unit
MEU(SOC)	Marine expeditionary unit (special operations capable)
MIA	missing in action
MILSTRIP	Military Standard Requisition and Issue Procedure
MK	mark
MLG	Marine logistics group
MMS	Marine mammal system
MOB	mobile
MOD	module
MOOTW	military operations other than war
MSCA	military support to civil authorities
MTTP	multi-Service tactics, techniques, and procedures
MWSG	Marine wing support group
MWSS	Marine wing support squadron

N

NARP	Nuclear Weapon Accident Response Procedures
NAVEODTECHDIV	Naval EOD Technology Division
NAVFOR	Navy Forces
NAVSCOLEOD	naval school explosive ordnance disposal
NAVSUP	Navy Supplement
NCO	noncommissioned officer
NEO	noncombatant evacuation operation
NRF	naval reserve force
NSSE	National Security Special Events
NSWRON	Naval Special Warfare Squadron
NWDC	Navy Warfare Development Command

O

OCD	ordnance clearance detachment
OCONUS	outside the continental United States
OD	ordnance
OPCON	operational control
OPLAN	operation plan
OPORD	operation order
OPR	office of primary responsibility

P

PAO	public affairs officer
POC	point of contact
POTUS	President of the United States
POW	prisoner of war
PRETECHREP	preliminary technical report
PSD	Personnel Security Details

R

RAC	Radiological Accident
RCT	rescue coordination team
REDHORSE	Rapid Engineers Deployable Heavy Operations Repair Squadron, Engineers
REMOTECH	Andros Operations and Maintenance
RSP	render safe procedures

S

SASO	support and stability operations
SCUBA	self-contained underwater breathing apparatus
SHORE	shore-based
SJA	Staff Judge Advocate
SMCM	surface mine countermeasures
SNCO	staff noncommissioned officer
SOF	special operations forces
SOFA	status-of-forces agreement
SOP	standard operating procedure
SPIE	specialized personnel insertion/extraction
SRC	survival recovery center

T

TACON	tactical control
TECHINT	technical intelligence
TF	task force
TPFDD	time-phased force and deployment data
TRADOC	US Army Training and Doctrine command
TRAP	tactical recovery of aircraft and personnel (Marine Corps)
TTP	tactics, techniques, and procedures

U

UMCM	underwater mine countermeasures
USSS	United States Secret Service (Department of the Treasury)
UTC	unit type code
UXO	unexploded explosive ordnance

V

VBSS	visit, board, search, and seizure
VIP	very important person
VIPPSA	very important person protection support activity
VPOTUS	Vice President of the United States
VSW	very shallow water

W

WMD	weapons of mass destruction

PART II – TERMS AND DEFINITIONS

administrative control - Direction or exercise of authority over subordinate or other organizations in respect to administration and support, including organization of Service forces, control of resources and equipment, personnel management, unit logistics, individual and unit training, readiness, mobilization, demobilization, discipline, and other matters not included in the operational missions of the subordinate or other organizations. Also called ADCON. (JP 1-02)

aerial port of debarkation - An airfield for sustained air movement at which personnel and materiel are discharged from aircraft. Aerial ports of debarkation normally serve as ports of embarkation for return passengers and retrograde cargo shipments. Also called APOD. (FM 55-1)

aerial port of embarkation - An airfield for sustained air movement at which personnel and materiel board or are loaded aboard aircraft to initiate aerial movement. Aerial ports of embarkation may serve as ports of debarkation for return passengers and retrograde cargo shipments. Also called APOE. (FM 55-1)

alliance - An alliance is the result of formal agreements (i.e., treaties) between two or more nations for broad, long-term objectives that further the common interests of the members. (JP 1-02)

area of operations - An operational area defined by the joint force commander for land and naval forces. Areas of operation do not typically encompass the entire operational area of the joint force commander, but should be large enough for component commanders to accomplish their missions and protect their forces. Also called AO. (JP 1-02)

area of responsibility - The geographical area associated with a combatant command within which a combatant commander has authority to plan and conduct operations. Also called AOR. (JP 1-02)

assign - 1. To place units or personnel in an organization where such placement is relatively permanent, and/or where such organization controls and administers the units or personnel for the primary function, or greater portion of the functions, of the unit or personnel. 2. To detail individuals to specific duties or functions where such duties or functions are primary and/or relatively permanent. (JP 1-02)

attach - 1. The placement of units or personnel in an organization where such placement is relatively temporary. 2. The detailing of individuals to specific functions where such functions are secondary or relatively temporary, e.g., attached for quarters and rations; attached for flying duty. (JP 1-02)

battalion - A unit consisting of two or more company-, battery-, or troop-sized units and a headquarters. Also called BN. (FM 3-90)

brigade - A unit usually smaller than a division to which are attached groups and/or battalions and smaller units tailored to meet anticipated requirements. Also called BDE. (JP 1-02)

coalition - An ad hoc arrangement between two or more nations for common action. (JP 1-02)

combatant command - A unified or specified command with a broad continuing mission under a single commander established and so designated by the President, through the Secretary of Defense and with the advice and assistance of the Chairman of the Joint Chiefs of Staff. Combatant commands typically have geographic or functional responsibilities. (JP 1-02)

combatant commander - A commander of one of the unified or specified combatant commands established by the President. (JP 1-02)

command and control - The exercise of authority and direction by a properly designated commander over assigned and attached forces in the accomplishment of the mission. Command and control functions are performed through an arrangement of personnel, equipment, communications, facilities, and procedures employed by a commander in planning, directing, coordinating, and controlling forces and operations in the accomplishment of the mission. Also called C2. (JP 1-02)

commander, amphibious task force - The Navy officer designated in the order initiating the amphibious operation as the commander of the amphibious task force. Also called CATF. (JP 1-02)

common servicing - That function performed by one Military Service in support of another Military Service for which reimbursement is not required from the Service receiving support. (JP 1-02)

company - A unit consisting of two or more platoons, usually of the same type, with a headquarters and a limited capacity for self-support. Also called CO. (FM 3-90)

continental United States - United States territory, including the adjacent territorial waters, located within North America between Canada and Mexico. Also called CONUS. (JP 1-02)

contingency plan - A plan for major contingencies that can reasonably be anticipated in the principal geographic subareas of the command. (JP 1-02)

date-time group - The date and time, expressed in digits and time zone suffix, at which the message was prepared for transmission. (Expressed as six digits followed by the time zone suffix; first pair of digits denotes the date, second pair the hours, third pair the minutes, followed by a three-letter month abbreviation and two-digit year abbreviation.) Also called DTG. (JP 1-02)

direct liaison authorized - That authority granted by a commander (any level) to a subordinate to directly consult or coordinate an action with a command or agency within or outside of the granting command. Direct liaison authorized is more applicable to planning than operations and always carries with it the requirement of keeping the commander granting direct liaison authorized informed. Direct liaison authorized is a coordination relationship, not an authority through which command may be exercised. Also called DIRLAUTH. (JP 1-02)

direct support - A mission requiring a force to support another specific force and authorizing it to answer directly to the supported force's request for assistance. Also called DS. (JP 1-02)

executive agent - A term used to indicate a delegation of authority by the Secretary of Defense to a subordinate to act on the Secretary's behalf. An agreement between equals does not create an executive agent. For example, a Service cannot become a Department of Defense executive agent for a particular matter with simply the agreement of the other Services; such authority must be delegated by the Secretary of Defense. Designation as executive agent, in and of itself, confers no authority. The exact nature and scope of the authority delegated must be stated in the document designating the executive agent. An executive agent may be limited to providing only administration and support or coordinating common functions, or it may be delegated authority, direction, and control over specified resources for specified purposes. Also called EA. (JP 1-02)

explosive ordnance - All munitions containing explosives, nuclear fission or fusion materials, and biological and chemical agents. This includes bombs and warheads; guided and ballistic missiles; artillery, mortar, rocket, and small arms ammunition; all mines, torpedoes, and depth charges; demolition charges; pyrotechnics; clusters and dispensers; cartridge and propellant actuated devices; electro-explosive devices; clandestine and improvised explosive devices; and all similar or related items or components explosive in nature. (JP 1-02)

explosive ordnance disposal - The detection, identification, on-site evaluation, rendering safe, recovery, and final disposal of unexploded explosive ordnance. It may also include explosive ordnance which has become hazardous by damage or deterioration. Also called EOD. (JP 1-02)

functional component command - A command normally, but not necessarily, composed of forces of two or more Military Departments which may be established across the range of military operations to perform particular operational missions that may be of short duration or may extend over a period of time. (JP 1-02)

general support - That support which is given to the supported force as a whole and not to any particular subdivision thereof. Also called GS. (JP 1-02)

general support-reinforcing - General support-reinforcing artillery has the mission of supporting the force as a whole and of providing reinforcing forces for other artillery units. Also called GSR. (FM 101-5)

group - A flexible administrative and tactical unit composed of either two or more battalions or two or more squadrons. The term also applies to combat support and combat service support units. Also called GP. (FM 3-4.111)

humanitarian demining - Department of Defense and Department of State program to promote the foreign policy interests of the United States by assisting other nations in protecting their populations from landmines and clearing land of the threat posed by landmines remaining after conflict has ended. The humanitarian demining program includes training of host nation deminers, establishment of national demining organizations, provision of demining equipment, mine awareness training, and research development. (JP 1-02)

improvised explosive device - A device placed or fabricated in an improvised manner incorporating destructive, lethal, noxious, pyrotechnic, or incendiary chemicals and designed to destroy, incapacitate, harass, or distract. It may incorporate military stores, but is normally devised from nonmilitary components. Also called IED. (JP 1-02)

interoperability - 1. The ability of systems, units, or forces to provide services to and accept services from other systems, units, or forces and to use the services so exchanged to enable them to operate effectively together. 2. (DOD only) The condition achieved among communications-electronics systems or items of communications-electronics equipment when information or services can be exchanged directly and satisfactorily between them and/or their users. The degree of interoperability should be defined when referring to specific cases. (JP 1-02)

joint force commander - A general term applied to a combatant commander, subunified commander, or joint task force commander authorized to exercise combatant command (command authority) or operational control over a joint force. Also called JFC. (JP 1-02)

joint force land component commander - The commander within a unified command, subordinate unified command, or joint task force responsible to the establishing commander for making recommendations on the proper employment of assigned, attached, and/or made available for tasking land forces; planning and coordinating land operations; or accomplishing such operational missions as may be assigned. The joint force land component commander is given the authority necessary to accomplish missions and tasks assigned by the establishing commander. Also called JFLCC. (JP 1-02)

joint operations - A general term to describe military actions conducted by joint forces or by Service forces in relationships (e.g., support, coordinating authority) which, of themselves, do not create joint forces. (JP 1-02)

joint operations area - An area of land, sea, and airspace, defined by a geographic combatant commander or subordinate unified commander, in which a joint force commander (normally a joint task force commander) conducts military operations to accomplish a specific mission. Joint operations areas are particularly useful when operations are limited in scope and geographic area or when operations are to be conducted on the boundaries between theaters. Also called JOA. (JP 1-02)

Joint Operation Planning and Execution System - A system that provides the foundation for conventional command and control by national- and combatant command-level commanders and their staffs. It is designed to satisfy their information needs in the conduct of joint planning and operations. Joint Operation Planning and Execution System (JOPES) includes joint operation planning policies, procedures, and reporting structures supported by communications and automated data processing systems. JOPES is used to monitor, plan, and execute mobilization, deployment, employment, sustainment, and redeployment activities associated with joint operations. Also called JOPES. (JP 1-02)

joint task force - A joint force that is constituted and so designated by the Secretary of Defense, a combatant commander, a subunified commander, or an existing joint task force commander. Also called JTF. (JP 1-02)

liaison - That contact or intercommunication maintained between elements of military forces or other agencies to ensure mutual understanding and unity of purpose and action. (JP 1-02)

logistic support - Logistic support encompasses the logistic services, materiel, and transportation required to support the continental United States-based and worldwide deployed forces. (JP 1-02)

Marine air-ground task force - The Marine Corps principal organization for all missions across the range of military operations, composed of forces task-organized under a single commander capable of responding rapidly to a contingency anywhere in the world. The types of forces in the Marine air-ground task force (MAGTF) are functionally grouped into four core elements: a command element, an aviation combat element, a ground combat element, and a combat service support element. The four core elements are categories of forces, not formal commands. The basic structure of the MAGTF never varies, though the number, size, and type of Marine Corps units comprising each of its four elements will always be mission dependent. The flexibility of the organizational structure allows for one or more subordinate MAGTFs to be assigned. Also called MAGTF. (JP 1-02)

Marine expeditionary unit - A Marine air-ground task force (MAGTF) that is constructed around an infantry battalion reinforced, a helicopter squadron reinforced, and a task-organized combat service support element. It normally fulfills Marine Corps forward sea-based deployment requirements. The Marine expeditionary unit provides an immediate reaction capability for crisis response and is capable of limited combat operations. Also called MEU. (JP 1-02)

Marine expeditionary unit (special operations capable) - The Marine Corps standard, forward-deployed, sea-based expeditionary organization. The Marine expeditionary unit (special operations capable) (MEU[SOC]) is a Marine expeditionary unit, augmented with selected personnel and equipment, that is trained and equipped with an enhanced capability to conduct amphibious operations and a variety of specialized missions of limited scope and duration. These capabilities include specialized demolition, clandestine reconnaissance and surveillance, raids, in-extremis hostage recovery, and enabling operations for follow-on forces. The MEU(SOC) is not a special operations force but, when directed by the Secretary of Defense, the combatant commander, and/or other operational commander, may conduct limited special operations in extremis, when other forces are inappropriate or unavailable. Also called MEU(SOC). (JP 1-02)

military operations other than war - Operations that encompass the use of military capabilities across the range of military operations short of war. These military actions can be applied to complement any combination of the other instruments of national power and occur before, during, and after war. Also called MOOTW. (JP 1-02)

Military Service - A branch of the Armed Forces of the United States, established by act of Congress, in which persons are appointed, enlisted, or inducted for military service, and which operates and is administered within a military or executive department. The Military Services are: the United States Army, the United States Navy, the United States Air Force, the United States Marine Corps, and the United States Coast Guard. (JP 1-02)

mine - 1. In land mine warfare, an explosive or material, normally encased, designed to destroy or damage ground vehicles, boats, or aircraft, or designed to wound, kill, or otherwise incapacitate personnel. It may be detonated by the action of its victim, by the passage of time, or by controlled means. 2. In naval mine warfare, an explosive device laid in the water with the intention of damaging or sinking ships or of deterring shipping from entering an area. The term does not include devices attached to the bottoms of ships or to harbor installations by personnel operating underwater, nor does it include devices which explode immediately on expiration of a predetermined time after laying. (JP 1-02)

multinational - Between two or more forces or agencies of two or more nations or coalition partners. (JP 1-02)

munition - A complete device charged with explosives, propellants, pyrotechnics, initiating composition, or nuclear, biological, or chemical material for use in military operations, including demolitions. Certain suitably modified munitions can be used for training, ceremonial, or nonoperational purposes. Also called ammunition. (Note: In common usage, "munitions" [plural] can be military weapons, ammunition, and equipment.) (JP 1-02)

noncombatant evacuation operations - Operations directed by the Department of State, the Department of Defense, or other appropriate authority whereby noncombatants are evacuated from foreign countries when their lives are endangered by war, civil unrest, or natural disaster to safe havens or to the United States. Also called NEOs. (JP 1-02)

nuclear weapon - A complete assembly (i.e., implosion type, gun type, or thermonuclear type), in its intended ultimate configuration which, upon completion of the prescribed arming, fusing, and firing sequence, is capable of producing the intended nuclear reaction and release of energy. (JP 1-02)

operational control - Command authority that may be exercised by commanders at any echelon at or below the level of combatant command. Operational control is inherent in combatant command (command authority) and may be delegated within the command. When forces are transferred between combatant commands, the command relationship the gaining commander will exercise (and the losing commander will relinquish) over these forces must be specified by the Secretary of Defense. Operational control is the authority to perform those functions of command over subordinate forces involving organizing and employing commands and forces, assigning tasks, designating objectives, and giving authoritative direction necessary to accomplish the mission. Operational control includes authoritative direction over all aspects of military operations and joint training necessary to accomplish missions assigned to the command. Operational control should be exercised through the commanders of subordinate organizations. Normally this authority is exercised through subordinate joint force commanders and Service and/or functional component commanders. Operational control normally provides full authority to organize commands and forces and to employ those forces as the commander in operational control considers necessary to accomplish assigned missions; it does not, in and of itself, include authoritative direction for logistics or matters of administration, discipline, internal organization, or unit training. Also called OPCON. (JP 1-02)

operations center - The facility or location on an installation, base, or facility used by the commander to command, control, and coordinate all crisis activities. (JP 1-02)

ordnance - Explosives, chemicals, pyrotechnics, and similar stores, e.g., bombs, guns and ammunition, flares, smoke, or napalm. (JP 1-02)

recovery - 1. In air (aviation) operations, that phase of a mission which involves the return of an aircraft to a land base or platform afloat. 2. The retrieval of a mine from the location where emplaced. 3. Actions taken to rescue or extract personnel for return to friendly control. 4. Actions taken to extricate damaged or disabled equipment for return to friendly control or repair at another location. (JP 1-02)

Service component command - A command consisting of the Service component commander and all those Service forces, such as individuals, units, detachments, organizations, and installations under that command, including the support forces that have been assigned to a combatant command or further assigned to a subordinate unified command or joint task force. (JP 1-02)

special operations forces - Those Active and Reserve Component forces of the Military Services designated by the Secretary of Defense and specifically organized, trained, and equipped to conduct and support special operations. Also called SOF. (JP 1-02)

status-of-forces agreement - An agreement that defines the legal position of a visiting military force deployed in the territory of a friendly state. Agreements delineating the status of visiting military forces may be bilateral or multilateral. Provisions pertaining to the status of visiting forces may be set forth in a separate agreement, or they may form a part of a more comprehensive agreement. These provisions describe how the authorities of a visiting force may control members of that force and the amenability of the force or its members to the local law or to the authority of local officials. To the extent that agreements delineate matters affecting the relations between a military force and civilian authorities and population, they may be considered as civil affairs agreements. Also called SOFA. (JP 1-02)

submunition - Any munition that, to perform its task, separates from a parent munition. (JP 1-02)

tactical control - Command authority over assigned or attached forces or commands, or military capability or forces made available for tasking, that is limited to the detailed direction and control of movements or maneuvers within the operational area necessary to accomplish missions or tasks assigned. Tactical control is inherent in operational control. Tactical control may be delegated to, and exercised at any level at or below the level of combatant command. When forces are transferred between combatant commands, the command relationship the gaining commander will exercise (and the losing commander will relinquish) over these forces must be specified by the Secretary of Defense. Tactical control provides sufficient authority for controlling and directing the application of force or tactical use of combat support assets within the assigned mission or task. Also called TACON. (JP 1-02)

task force - 1. A temporary grouping of units, under one commander, formed for the purpose of carrying out a specific operation or mission. 2. A semi-permanent organization of units, under one commander, formed for the purpose of carrying out a continuing specific task. 3. A component of a fleet organized by the commander of a task fleet or higher authority for the accomplishment of a specific task or tasks. Also called TF. (JP 1-02)

time-phased force and deployment data - The Joint Operation Planning and Execution System database portion of an operation plan; it contains time-phased force data, non-unit-related cargo and personnel data, and movement data for the operation plan, including the following: a. In-place units; b. Units to be deployed to support the operation plan with a priority indicating the desired sequence for their arrival at the port of debarkation; c. Routing of forces to be deployed; d. Movement data associated with deploying forces; e. Estimates of non-unit-related cargo and personnel movements to be conducted concurrently with the deployment of forces; and f. Estimate of transportation requirements that must be fulfilled by common-user lift resources as well as those requirements that can be fulfilled by assigned or attached transportation resources. Also called TPFDD. (JP 1-02)

unexploded explosive ordnance - Explosive ordnance which has been primed, fused, armed or otherwise prepared for action, and which has been fired, dropped, launched, projected, or placed in such a manner as to constitute a hazard to operations, installations, personnel, or material and remains unexploded either by malfunction or design or for any other cause. Also called UXO. (JP 1-02)

unit type code - A Joint Chiefs of Staff developed and assigned code, consisting of five characters that uniquely identify a "type unit." (JP 1-02)

weapons of mass destruction - Weapons that are capable of a high order of destruction and/or of being used in such a manner as to destroy large numbers of people. Weapons of mass destruction can be high explosives or nuclear, biological, chemical, and radiological weapons, but exclude the means of transporting or propelling the weapon where such means is a separable and divisible part of the weapon. Also called WMD. (JP 1-02)

INDEX

FM 4-30.16
MCRP 3-17.2C
NTTP 3-02.5
AFTTP(I) 3-2.32

27 October 2005

By Order of the Secretary of the Army:

Official:

PETER J. SCHOOMAKER
General, United States Army
Chief of Staff

Sandra R. Riley

SANDRA R. RILEY
Administrative Assistant to the
Secretary of the Army
     0531102

DISTRIBUTION:
Active Army, Army National Guard, and US Army Reserve. To be distributed in accordance with IDN 115839, requirements for FM 4-30.16.

By Order of the Secretary of the Air Force

BENTLEY B. RAYBURN
Major General, USAF
Commander
Headquarters Air Force Doctrine Center

Air Force Distribution: F
Supersedes AFTTP(I) 3-2.32, 15 February 2001.

www.ingramcontent.com/pod-product-compliance
Lightning Source LLC
Chambersburg PA
CBHW081119290526
45795CB00006B/2179